The Perfect Girl, The Prostitute, & Other Stories

CC ADETULA

This book is a work of fiction. The characters, incidents, and dialogue are drawn from the author's imagination and are not to be construed as real. Any resemblance to actual events or persons, living or dead, is entirely coincidental.

THE PERFECT GIRL, THE PROSTITUTE, &

OTHER STORIES.

Published by StorySheWrote Media
Ellicott City, MD
USA
storyshewrotemedia@gmail.com

Amazon Reviews of *The Perfect Girl*

"CC Adetula is a fresh voice with the mastery of a veteran. She takes the writer on a really smooth journey complete with the thrills that come with riding a well oiled roller coaster. Writing with a flair that is uniquely hers, her short stories take you through different tastes and climes."

"I just bought more copies of this book to give as Christmas gifts. I'm not usually a fan of short stories, because they always leave me wanting more, and this book did that, but the way in which the author left me wanting more was rich, and evocative..."

"In reading this book, I realized that I have sort of come to expect 'African' writers of fiction to write in a certain 'way' about a certain, predictable set of issues. After reading The Perfect Girl, I have had to totally revise my impression. It was such a refreshingly different sort of book to read. I really hope I'll have the chance to read another book by this gifted author soon!"

"Her mastery of language left me with a feeling of sophistication and relate-ability. Her words literally leapt off the page and had me wanting more."

"For a first time author, C.C. Adetula is bold, courageous and quite adventurous."

"...One cannot help but admire Adetula's sense of imagination. Her creative impulse, her eyes for even the minutest detail, the imagery, the nuances, and her mastery of the story telling skills arrest the reader's attention and keep the reader captive in a pleasant way till the last page."

"... is a breath of fresh air. The way she tells her stories is captivating, imaginative and fun! This book is a must-read....can't wait for the next one."

"A tightly written series of short stories from a Nigerian woman's perspective that even an "oyibo" man can enjoy."

"CC Adetula is a very talented author and I believe this marks the beginning of a long and fruitful writing career."

"Her mastery of language left me with a feeling of sophistication and relate-ability. Her words literally leapt off the page and had me wanting more."

"CC Adetula has mastery of story telling which keeps the reader glued to the page. She has a way of weaving details into a rich tapestry which ignites curiosity and is completely absorbing. Each story is engrossing and leaves the reader with a sense of satisfaction and looking forward to the next tale."

"....Truly amazing short stories. Just enough to wet your whistle while keeping you intrigued to theorize what could have happened next."

"The realism and humanity her characters represent made you feel like... "this could be me," I loved the nuggets and glimpses into the Nigerian heritage and customs - enough to understand not too much to confuse but applicable to my western upbringing."

"...An entertaining and thought provoking read which fuses the art of African storytelling with carefully selected contemporary diction that keeps the reader engaged to the end of each story."

" I am simply amazed at how the author can make you fall in love with a character in only a few short pages."

" From the first page, the author ... drew me in with her witty anecdotes and colorful storytelling, I didn't realize I was turning pages until I was halfway through the book!!"

"...A beautiful, well written book that is balanced, intriguing and so unique. "

"This book gave me a lot to think about. I did not want the stories to end as I knew I would want more. Each story evoked a different emotion from me."

Dedicated to the memory of My Father – the much revered past,

AND

My children – the insanely brilliant future.

I am extremely proud of both. I have been greatly blessed by both.

Contents

The Sister

I used to be beautiful. I tell you, child, I used to be awesome and all that - with my half nappy buck shots and teased tips, at the mercy of whatever leftover relaxer I could coax from my mother or however much I could steal from her purse, fast like lightning, when she left the room. I was fierce in my friend's hand-me-downs - particularly a pair of billowing culottes, three sizes too big, with the matching top that was slightly faded because my best friend Ogechi had particularly liked the 'slashed' shirt.Just like Paula Abdul, she said, and she had worn it incessantly, in and out of season, before she relinquished it to me reluctantly. In addition to being faded, it was, like its bottom half, also about two or three sizes too big and would slip over my shoulder. So there I was, resplendent (or so I thought) in my faded, too big clothes, *shrugging my left shoulder every six seconds, self imposed nervous twitch intact.*

*** *** ***

Dear Lord, but my little sister is gorgeous! She is petite, 5'3" to my long, lanky 6', with my mother's face and laugh - *Oh Mother mine*-chocolate insouciance all her own. She is tapping her impossibly tiny, leather boot-clad foot, in that impatient, yet endearing way she has.

Her back is turned towards me, the word 'Juicy" brazenly emblazoned on her behind, and I just stand for a minute drinking her in. She was only six when I left home, complete with runny nose and little, hard, threaded plaits, clinging to our mother's wrapper. And I had the same lump in my throat then as I do now, picking her up from the airport ten years later. She had asked how I would recognize her and I had chuckled at the thought of not recognizing Uzo. Even without the myriad of pictures she had bombarded me with over the years (is that all they did in Nigeria now, take pictures?), she couldn't have been anybody else, not with Mother's face and stance, right leg slightly bent, hand on hip. Besides, she was dressed to the nines in typical Nigerian fashion. Complete with denim jacket and "juicy couture" bottoms. How can she afford it? I do a mental conversion of dollars to naira in my head and I still cannot fathom her sudden fortune, a far cry from Ogechi's hand-me-down culottes.

I sweep her up from behind and swing her around. For a split second I see panic written in her round, impossibly big yet ridiculously gorgeous eyes and in the perfect 'O' of her pouty lips. "Nwanne!" she screams. *Sister*. Those two syllables are steeped in love, respect and pure utter joy in recognizing the familiar. Borrowed western poise is momentarily forgotten and meticulously rehearsed affectations are erased. For a brief moment, she is four again and I am the protector of my little sister in the inevitable tussles that occur among children, squabbling in the sand. "Hiiiiiiiiiiiiiiiiiiiiiii!" She has composed herself and is determined to implement the vivacious "Americanized" greeting that she has seen in so many movies back home. She pulls my head down and kisses me, almost too vigorously, on both cheeks. *Wrong continent for that, darling*, I think to myself wryly. The miniscule malicious satisfaction I get from her gaucheness quickly dissipates when I realize that Uzo has what I will never possess - the brazenness to be *who* she wants to be, *when* she wants to be it.

Yes indeed, this child is something to behold.

*** *** ***

But seriously, what happened to 'not speaking until you were spoken to?' and not looking your elders in the eyes when you spoke to them? It is an art, you see, striking the delicate balance between being respectful and trying not to appear shifty and up to no good. You had to get the tone of voice and the inflection just right - an octave too high and you would come off as belligerent, too low would mean that you were deliberately muffling your words because you were telling lies and did not wish to be found out.

I had mastered this art early on and could worm my way into the most coveted sanctuaries of the 'grown-ups'. Brother Ejike was not quite an adult like Mother and Father, but he had hair on his chest, his own sleeping quarters and rarely had to do any chores. He was my Father's half brother's only son, whom my father had taken in when his father passed away and was adored by everybody. I used to lie on Ejike's bed, pretending to be asleep and listening to he and his friends talk about the girls they had 'had', and the girls they would have when they went to University.

Everyone knew that girls loved the "Umu University". Even the village girls, unexposed and unsophisticated as they were, knew the difference. Take Azuka, for instance, one of the few village belles that refused to fool around with my brother when we came to the village for Christmas or the New Yam festival. Once she learned that Ejike had received his Joint Admission and Matriculation Board Results and that he could possibly receive a scholarship to study 'overseas', she started coming over to the house in the evenings. So much so that Mother would contort her face disapprovingly and in a loud voice ask her, "Mama gi kwanu?" - "How is your mother?" This was code for "I know your mother and if you misbehave with my son, you can be sure she'll hear about it." It always worked like a charm and Azuka would go scurrying into the night like a startled doe, much to Ejike's chagrin. But she would be back, unable to help herself, in what seemed like the same exact spot the next day.

*** *** ***

On our drive from the airport home, she is chatting animatedly, one million miles per minute. Dear Lord, I think to myself, is this who I was at sixteen? Invincible master and conqueror of jet lag even while a gazillion miles from home, completely comfortable with a sister I barely knew or remembered? I drive with a smile plastered on my face, only half listening, and trying desperately to collect my thoughts. When I was sixteen, what did I like to talk about? I am drawing blanks, maybe because I was never sixteen, not in the way that Uzo is now. It doesn't seem to matter though - Uzo seems adept at conducting one sided conversations. "...So this is America, huh? It's just like Lagos..."- blasé and controlled this one is- "...I don't see what the big deal is anyway? You would think that it is not the same oxygen we breathe in Nigeria..." *You would, indeed*, and having been through hell to bring her here, I feel slightly peeved. Childishly, I am tempted to tell her that a flight back to Nigeria can easily be arranged. But I hold back. It is her first day here and I am, after all, the elder by a good ten years.

*** *** ***

On the eve of my departure from Nigeria, the house had been packed full with everyone who had known me (and some who had no idea who I was) from my childhood up until then. In anticipation of this event my father had borrowed chairs from the 'Center,' the 'Hall-of-All Trades' that was used for every activity you could think of -weddings, child dedications, town meetings-. I was the first of my father's children to have gone "overseas" as we referred to it back then, so this was a major deal. Before me there had been Brother Ejike of course, but no one really spoke of him anymore. He had gone to Russia on a scholarship to study Medicine but ended up marrying his host family's daughter - Sveta was her name, I think - and had subsequently dropped out of school and started to run his new father-in- law's business. We rarely heard from him after that and if my parents communicated with him at all, it was never shared with us. He had "missed road" or 'defected' as it were, was obviously an ingrate and had proven unworthy of the love and care Father had showered on him since infancy. It was my duty now to undo his unspeakable wrongdoings, my Mother had told me in a matter of fact manner. I could not forget where I came from even though I was a woman who would one day marry and leave her Father's house. The women from my mother's group at church gathered round saying 'novenas'for my trip, and the more traditional well wishers muttered affirmations under their breath while sipping the local gin. Although Ejike's name was not mentioned, it hung in the air. All through the night, the refrain was the same - "You will be a good ambassador of your people in 'obodo oyibo' (white man's land)." "You will not forget your parents or your siblings or the good things they have taught you, *enu*?" *Enu*? You hear? It was a rhetorical question but I still nodded meekly. It did not matter that I had never given them cause to think otherwise of me. One just accepted the reverse negative prayers in the spirit in which they were intended.

*** *** ***

I attempt a conversation, deliberately speaking in Igbo as if to make sure that this girl whom I just picked up from the airport with the lip gloss and the shiny, badly sewn in hair extensions, is indeed my little sister, an authentic Igbo girl, despite the imitation Louis Vuitton hand bag. "So... what did you do on your last day in Nigeria? Did Daddy have the huge send off and the prayers at the house and the airport? I remember mine, it was so embarrassing..." She cuts me off, answering in English, "Oh...please... He let me have a party with my friends from school and Daddy had the driver take me to the airport." I pause, trying to reconcile the family that I left behind and the 'Huxtable' household it has morphed into. I cannot fathom my father letting any of us leave the country without the obligatory prayers and advice from friends and family. I remember finding some of the advice from the numerous family and friends that filled our house on the eve of my departure ludicrous - "Make sure when you see someone else's corn, you do not take it and say it is your own," and "Always return the hoe that you borrowed from your neighbor and do not keep it as your own." They spoke figuratively I knew, but I found it absurd all the same. If Mother was still alive *(Mother, mother mine)* things would have been different for my sister, I'm sure. The night before my departure, Mother was in the kitchen, pounding, cooking and frying delicacies for me to eat on the plane. Mother never quite grasped the concept of how airlines worked. She knew that we were fed on the plane, but she was convinced that it would never be enough to tide me over for the fourteen hours that I would be flying. Everyone knew that the 'oyibo' served cold food - sandwiches with leaves and no hot pepper. She would pack me a flask with fried meat and some *puff-puff* and *chin-chin*, so that I would not throw up on the plane and disgrace the family. And then we had chuckled and I had cried a bit, because I was leaving home for the very first time, the next day.

Who would look after me now in this cold country called America? I barely knew the Aunt and Uncle I was being shipped off to. A lump rises in my throat — it has been almost ten years since my Mother passed, but some days, I can still smell her, feel her almost — and with Uzo here now, her resemblance to Mother makes my loss even more tangible. Uzo is looking at me curiously, so I frantically search for something to say. *Anything.* "Daddy has a driver now?" Uzo nods, "You know when we moved to Umuahia, they had to give him concessions for the relocation, so he asked for a new Peugeot with air conditioner and a driver..." Her lips are moving and I am responding with the obligatory smiles and attentive noises, but my thoughts are elsewhere.

*** *** ***

In the days leading up to my departure, I constantly alternated between different moods and emotions in an almost hormonal fashion, sad one minute and giddy the next. It was incredibly hard to leave the world as I knew it for another that the little I knew of had been gleaned from a few ancient re-runs of "Good Times" and "Different Strokes"that we watched on television when we could not get a signal for the network news. The rest of my information was part fable, part urban legend, interspersed with exaggerations and half-truths told by the few people I knew, who in turn knew someone who had actually lived in America. This was my nucleus, where I had my friends, family and routine. My best friend Ogechi and I would stay up for hours when she would sleep over at my house and talk way into the night about this fascinating adventure I was about to embark upon. You would think that I was Aladdin going on a 'magic carpet ride'. How far was America? Were the streets actually so clean that you could eat off them if you wanted to? What would I do in the winter? Did all the girls have nice clothes and long hair? Ogechi was convinced that once I went to the States, my hair would automatically grow longer and become more luxuriant. "It's the weather," she would say wisely, "and the food they eat -your skin will be like butter, and your hair will grow like that... fiam!" And she would snap for emphasis. I was not fully convinced, but I had no explanation for the way the girls looked, girls with skin as dark as mine, who could easily be from my villagebut for their accents. "When you come back, will I be able to understand you? You will start speaking through your nose like 'ndibekee'- Hia!" And I would get a playful smack on the arm. We would start giggling and then to console her we would talk about all the things I would buy for her once I got there. After all, everything was cheap in America - and not imitation 'Aba-made' cheap either. She wanted hair extensions, human hair ones that would fall to her waist, as well as the several pairs of the latest jeans and shoes. I was to come back to Nigeria at least once a year and the minute I was able to, send a plane ticket for her to visit. She could never live in America, she would say, shaking her head vigorously, as if she had been offered the opportunity. *Mba*! The cold was too much, and she knew she did not have the patience to try to decipher what these white people were saying. These were the same people who came and took our people as slaves, she would say accusingly, conveniently forgetting that just seconds before she had requested a plane ticket amongst other things from this country that she held in such disdain.

*** *** ***

All of a sudden I get it. We are not so different, Uzo and I. Underneath the bravado and worldliness, she was still just a little girl, the same age as I was when I left home, but a bit more sheltered in a weird way. If I was still reeling from the blow of losing Mother nine years later, then how must she have fared at seven, without me, without her mother? Who had taught her how to be a woman, girl things? She had been wrested from all she knew and had been taken to a strange place, to live with a sister she could barely remember. I look over at Uzo and she is now quiet, staring out the window. Dusk has fallen and the moon has just begun to peek from behind the clouds. "Nwanne?" I am startled almost by the plaintive quality in her voice. "Dalu." *Thank You*. She is still looking out the window, as if she might be speaking to someone outside of the car. Unsure of what exactly she is thanking me for, but understanding it on some intuitive, deeper level, I swallow the lump in my throat and reach over to rub her cheek gently.

She has come home.

The Runner

He'd seen her run by, once or twice - okay, maybe three or four times. She wore muted shades of pinks and purples, some aqua, and on the rare occasion, a neon and black spandex get-up; but mostly she wore pink, as if to brand her biological affiliation on her person. *Girl runner*, her racer-back screamed. *Female jogger*, her lavender laces chorused back. Then there were the ridiculous chignon styles she wore her hair in to run. Most serious female runners wore the headbands or their hair up on top of their heads in careless buns, like drunken ballerinas; but not her. She wore an assortment of clasps, barrettes and pins to secure the thick coronet of a braid she wore around her head. 'The running Tsarina,' Sophia had called her, aptly but not unkindly. Sophia was a 'serious' runner of the messy bun, no jewelry wearing variety–non-judgmental and welcoming of anyone who made an effort to run. At least they were trying, right? So score one for the runners community. The Tsarina also wore earrings and makeup, or at least looked like she did. Her cheeks were the perfect shade of light pink that seemed to come from a soupçon of blush, expensive enough not to look painted on and expertly applied to imitate sophisticated, tasteful exertion–more *Self* magazine than *Vogue*. Unlike say, Sophia, although that was hardly a fair comparison–Sophia made no effort at all. What he was trying to say, with no insult directed at Sophia and her ilk, was that runner girl Tsarina was beautiful. So beautiful that she looked like a 'poser' and everything she wore or did just seemed somehow a tad 'affected.'

He had a love-hate relationship with her; that is, if you could call their deliberate non-acknowledgement of each other a 'relationship'. That was another thing about her that irked him. Everyone knew about the 'runner's nod'- when running past another jogger, one nodded in acknowledgement. The nod said, "Hello, too physically exerted to speak, but I see ya!" *And good job braving these elements or terrain or conquering your laziness, whatever*. The nod was the 'Namaste' of the running world. But not to Ms. Hoity-toity Tsarina. No siree bob! She whizzed right past everyone with her inappropriately expensive windscreen-esque sunglasses. Who wore Versace sunglasses to run? Or regular sunglasses for that matter? He'd only noticed this because once, when they'd slid off her face and crashed onto the pavement, he had glanced at them briefly before he'd handed them back to her. She had given him an almost imperceptible nod of thanks, making sure their fingers did not graze as she took the glasses from him.

Bitch, he had thought to himself. Yet his stomach had tightened at the thought of her and his heart had done triple time when he'd seen her turning the corner the next day.

He'd unconsciously (of course) taken to running when she did. She ran on Monday, Wednesday and Friday mornings, right before it was really light out, before the hum of the high school buses and after the street lights had been switched off. He found that these times worked better for him also. There were fewer runners and familiar faces. One could really run with a clear head and not have to chat. Tsarina would run on the occasional Sunday as well, but she would run apart from the regulars – aloof in her pastels, fancy sunglasses and ridiculous braid.

"I'd like to see that one in a race," Sophia chortled, in between puffs of breath. He suddenly noticed with irritation what a noisy runner Sophia was. "I'm sure she'd do just fine." His tone was sharper than he'd intended. Sophia glanced at him strangely. "I mean, like using the porter potty. Or even drinking from a paper cup. Think she'd bring her own chalice?" Another rheumy chortle. He shrugged and picked up his pace ever so slightly–it felt disloyal somehow, to laugh at Tsarina, especially since they ran together now. Sort of.

He had started doing his warm up jog towards the direction of her house, stopping to stretch at lamp posts, breathing in the quiet, crisp morning air. By the time he got to her house, she was usually in her driveway, doing some kind of ridiculous yoga slash ballet poses; ridiculous, yet perfectly normal for her. If she noticed him she gave no sign of it, as she unhurriedly finished her routine; downward dog, warrior, cobra, tree pose, downward dog, tree pose. He played along, jogging past her well-manicured lawn–today there was a red tricycle on it–taking in the BMW and the Prius parked in the driveway. The BMW would be hers, of course; he had seen her zooming around in it. She'd had the top down, so she had been pretty hard to miss.

As he turned the corner to stretch again and wait a few minutes before running at a discreet distance behind her, he wondered like he usually did, about the Tsarina. What was she really like underneath the pastel wicking material? Behind the name brand accoutrements? What would it feel like to wake up next to her, to drive the blue Prius in the driveway, toss the tow-headed tricycle rider up in the air? He was not a lonely man or a stalker. Far from it. He was just intrigued by the Tsarina for some reason, the *idea* of her. He knew that once she finally acknowledged him, the spell would be over and the mystery dissipated, so he both dreaded and looked forward to it at the same time. He would not miss the getting up to run at the crack of dawn, but he was not sure he could bear the return to the humdrum routine of his life–the mid-morning runs with Sophia and the gang, and the conversations with his wife about what their boy Jeremy was up to in what country, and how else he should be spending his retirement.

"Running?" His wife had repeated dubiously, when he had initially told her he wanted to take it up. "I've never seen you so much as lace up a sneaker!" He cocked an eyebrow at her." You never saw me dance a jig or carry a golf club either, but that hasn't stopped you." She'd flushed, embarrassed at his reference to the slew of activities she had signed him up for the minute he got retired–cooking, ball room dancing, even Spanish classes at their local community college program for 55-plus citizens. "I was only trying to be helpful–" "Trying to keep my brain agile. Wouldn't want the old geezer to get a touch of 'the Alzheimer's' would we?" She winced. It was an unnecessary and undeserved jab at her and they both knew it. Her Dad was in a nursing home with full blown Alzheimer's and she worried, rightly so, about his condition. He pulled her in his arms and kissed her on the forehead swiftly. "I'm an ass. I'd really like to try running though. You should join me!" he said brightly, although they both knew she never would. Christine was many things, but runner or runner's wife she was not. She was capable and supportive wife, she had been class mom, and PTA secretary, school board member, dutiful daughter, glue of their family, but he just couldn't see her as one of the running group; she lacked the ability to be selfish and exercise just for her own benefit. Even her Zumbathons and Spin classes had purpose—Spin for leukemia, ALS awareness Zumba. She had done a mini triathlon once for a little boy with a congenital heart disease. He had died shortly after and the next week Christine had baked for his foundation fundraising. Supportive *and* purposeful, she definitely was.

He saw her run out of the corner of his eye and jogged behind her; just close enough so he could see her side profile, but with enough distance between them so as not to appear creepy. She was a rather noiseless runner; no puffing or loud controlled breaths. Her Swarovski crystal-studded ear buds did not leak sound, so he had no idea what she was listening to. Sophia had told him that a lot of women who ran alone had taken to not playing any music at all so that they would be fully aware of their surroundings. "What would be the point of the headphones, then?" he'd wondered, to which Sophia had responded cheerfully with a shrug, "Beats me."

She was not wearing her sunglasses this morning, since it was still pretty dark out. But she was wearing eye makeup; some sort of dark blue eye-shadow—wait no, it was a shiner! Someone had given the Tsarina a heck of a black eye. He felt the rage well up in him like embers of fire, the heat in his stomach slowly rising to his chest, making his heart wage war with his ribcage. That her despicable coward of a husband had hit her—what kind of a man would just clock a woman in the face? He had seen him a couple of times; washing the Prius, playing with the kid, mowing the lawn. Her husband had looked normal enough, but there was something about him he just couldn't stand—a smugness, or so. *Maybe that's because you wish you were him, because you want to be him*, a little voice inside him mocked. No, that was ridiculous! Although the Tsarina was not quite young enough to be his daughter, their age difference was still such that it would attract a decent amount of whispers and knowing glances.

Aside from her tightly clenched fists and bruised eye, she seemed like herself; ignoring him as usual, running with her unhurried stride, which really was faster than it seemed. He knew even before he had worked up the courage to clear his throat that asking her anything was a bad idea. They were neither friends, nor acquaintances. They were merely neighbors, in that suburban 2014 non-neighborly, no-eye-contact making way—no questions asked, maybe names and head nods of acknowledgment exchanged, maybe not. He and Tsarina weren't even that kind of 'neighbor close. But because he was an idiot, he asked her. Or attempted to, at least.

"So..."

"Get away from me, weirdo." The surprisingly husky timbre of her voice registered before the insult did. He flushed and sputtered out a response, "Excuse me?"

"I know your type–the anti-dirty old man, *dirty old man.* You don't fool me with your act. Well, it ain't gonna happen, grandpa."

She was flushed with the cold and perhaps a little anger, too. Perhaps she was mad at him for witnessing her vulnerability, so he would bear the brunt of her tongue lashing. Tears had filled her eyes. He noticed they were hazel and striking.

"Then why are you crying?" He asked softly. "Who's crying?" She wiped her eyes with the back of her sleeve with a fleeting half-smile. "Later, Pops." She quickened her pace and took off. He stared after her for as long as he could still make out her outline, and then when he could no longer see her, he jogged home slowly, not sure why, but smiling to himself.

On Wednesday she ignored him and had deviated from her normal route. He'd ignored her too, fake whistling in tune to the music he was fake listening to. He had snapped at Christine and she had said something about how she thought exercise was supposed to make you less grumpy. He had instantly felt remorse and had made it a point to be extra attentive to her needs that night. But he had thought of the Tsarina the whole time, resenting Christine a little for not being her, and hating himself for even thinking such unfair, foul, thoughts.

He'd deliberately delayed his running time the next morning and had gone late enough so she'd have left for work, but still early so as to avoid the 'real runners pack'. Sophia was just finishing her run and she glistened jubilantly with perspiration and achievement. "Seven miles before breakfast. Roohf!" She mock barked, raising a thin, yet muscular arm in a bicep flex. "You go girl! Lazy morning for me." She stuck her tongue out at him, "Well, you have the Duchess for company." At his confusion, she gestured, "You know, the Tsarina or whatever. Good luck with that!" And she was off with a smile.

He didn't turn around but he sensed and smelled her about the same time. She smelled lightly of lilies, which he liked.

"Don't ask, because we both know I won't answer." This was around when he noticed that she was holding her arm at an awkward angle. "It doesn't hurt that much when I keep it just so." Her voice was matter of fact, husky and flat.

"You need to report this to the police —" he began, indignation welling up in him.

"Yeah?" Her tone was derisive and mocking, "how are they gonna arrest the stairs I fell down?" she shook her head, "if you think he did this to me and I didn't report it, you need to put down that remote and back away from the Lifetime Movie channel, gramps."

He smiled at that because she would be right. He didn't know that much about her, but she was the unlikeliest victim of domestic abuse ever.

"Or maybe I should report you first, for stalking." She laughed and spun in the opposite direction from him, not looking back.

He froze for a minute, before he realized that of course she hadn't said that, or *any* of it, for that matter. There had been no conversation. She had laughed, yes, and she had turned to run in the other direction—but had she said that last thing about him stalking her? She hadn't spoken to him since their first brief encounter weeks ago, and she couldn't possibly have seen him looking through their kitchen window at night. He had only done it a couple of times; not up close of course—from the street.

It was easy to do, the way the houses were structured—at night everything was illuminated by the chandeliers, the lighting over-kill and flimsy blinds. Everyone did it, whether they admitted to it or not; it was just fun to see one's neighbor's decorating skills, or lack thereof. Heck, he'd even peeked in Sophia's house briefly,``one night, just for kicks. Plus, he was no *stalker*.

He did have to admit though, that it would be interesting to see how Tsarina's relationship was with her husband, particularly after the black eye and shoulder. He wasn't sure what he had thought he would see later that evening, but he'd felt oddly let down at their normalcy–their intimacy, even. They had eaten in the kitchen. Her husband had brought her a plate and they had chatted a bit, then she had cleared the table, while her husband had leaned against the fridge and they'd talked some more. He was convinced the husband *had* to be involved in the incident, he just wasn't sure *how*. He also knew that he should not get involved, but he couldn't help himself. Nothing good would come of his obsession, but he didn't want to stop.

She hadn't gone running the next week, or the week after that. He had walked by her house twice a day, looking for signs of vacation. The blinds were drawn, and on occasion a bedroom light would be on, but that was it. The BMW hadn't moved for weeks, he was sure of that, although he hadn't paid much attention to the Prius.

He approached Sophia and the real runners crew; he had been running alone these days, as it felt almost disloyal to run with them now–they still called her Tsarina and he felt a bit self-conscious telling them to stop.

"What's new?" He addressed Sophia and her sloppy bun. Sophia looked over at him soberly. "We should be asking you? Where's your girlfriend, the Duchess?"

"Who?" He was dumbfounded, at the fact that she was missing and he seemed to be the last to know, and also trying to process their assumptions that he would know her whereabouts. He didn't even know her name.

"Yeah, apparently some sicko's been watching her for months, tracking her movements, knew she ran alone and everything," Ted said a tad too casually, avoiding his gaze. Sophia opened her mouth and eyes really wide and shut them both, abruptly, like some kind of weird puppet. He decided then and there that he didn't like Ted or Sophia, at all—if he was to be perfectly honest, he probably never had. *They thought it was him. The bastards actually thought he might have something to do with her disappearance.*

"The police are going to want to talk to whoever might have seen her last; they've got to eliminate the husband as a suspect first, of course..." Ted was warming up to his retired cop spiel. But all he could think about was his overwhelming sense of loss—no more pinks and purples, no more lavender laces. Somewhere in the back of his mind, he wondered what kind of pie Christine would bake to take over to the Tsarina's family.

{3}

The Nanny

She sat in the large foyer, nervous, in the exact same spot the unsmiling housekeeper had shown her to moments before. She trembled slightly, but not from the cold; getting the job just meant way too much to her. It would mean heat in the winter and food on the table, as well as other comforts that she could only dream of back home in Mexico. *Diosmio*, how she wanted, no, needed, this job! She glanced down at her outfit, a black and white patterned dress with dark stockings, half obscured by the plain cloth black coat and matching scarf that she always wore around her neck. Dress to impress, the lady from the agency had said. Well, this was about as impressive as it got for her. The lady with the large glasses from the agency had also told her frankly, but not unkindly, that this was the last interview they would send her on, as she was proving "rather difficult to place." She stroked her throat, unconsciously fingering her scar as she often did when she was nervous. And nervous she was.

Mrs. Broadwater walked in, tall, blonde and impeccably groomed in that Manhattan, rich kind of way. "Grisela, is it? Did I say it right, Gree-seh-lah?" She talked a mile a minute, almost like she was the nervous one. This reassured Grisela and she relaxed a bit. "*Si Senora.*"

Oh, Mrs. Broadwater (or Kath, as she had insisted) leading her into what looked like the formal living room, full of over-stuffed sofas and paintings, mostly of young children and cocker spaniels. "This is a beautiful house, *Senora.*" Kath waved a hand at her in the nervous impatient way she had, brushing aside her compliment and motioning for herto sit all at the same time. "It's Kath, please." She pointed to the canvases on the wall. "I painted most of these – you like?" She flashed her eager smile again.

"Cliff, my husband," - again that slight wave - "calls it my stress outlet, but I'll tell you a little secret - I just love to do it, stressed or not. Sssshh, that stays between us, okay?" She smiled at Grisela, delighted, as if they had just shared some delicious naughty secret together. "They are beautiful." Grisela hesitated, she could not bring herself to call her Kath, so she fell silent again. Kath smiled again, not just a mere flash this time, exposing her impossibly perfect veneers. "I knew I liked you for a reason." She played with a cigarette absentmindedly. "Can never find any fricking ashtrays in this place. Cliff wants me to give up smoking so he hides them.And Aida," she glanced over her shoulder, lowering her voice as if afraid of being overheard by the housekeeper. "Aida, she's on his side, you know. Me against them. So, another secret. This house has more secrets than the fucking CIA, you know?" Her tone was matter-of-fact as if she hadn't just dropped the 'f-bomb', but she grinned, self-deprecating, "Sure you still want to work for us, Grisela?"

Grisela stared at her and nodded slowly while reaching into her bag for an empty plastic bottle. It said 'Sunny-D' orange juice on the worn label. "Ashtray?" She handed it to Kath. Another genuine mega watt smile. "You, my dear, are a wonder." Kath enveloped Grisela in a hug, leaving her smelling faintly of rosewater and cigarettes. "What can I say Grisela, you've got the job!" Again, a flash of the veneers, "Cliff will probably have a mini cow, but who the hell cares, no?"

Grisela swallowed hard, barely comprehending, "*Si...gracias...*"She often reverted to her native tongue in her confusion. Kath was barely listening, flushed and enthused by her own impulsiveness. "Of course you'll have to stay and meet Kimmie – she gets back from school in about half an hour. She will adore you, I'm sure of it. And it will be nice to have her speaking Spanish again..." She clasped her hand over her mouth. "Oh my gosh, let me take your coat - I know, a mere thirty minutes later." She made a moue at her lack of hostessing skills and tugged at Grisela's coat. Grisela watched immobile as the loosely knotted scarf came undone leaving her scar exposed, a crude thick line across her throat. "Oh..." Kath's mouth was a perfect circle as she searched for the appropriate words; they never came. Grisela spoke softly, but rapidly, tears rolling down her face. "He said he would kill me, but I never believed him. My husband, he..." snuffling she accepted the handkerchief that was wordlessly offered,"...he was drunk and angry, like a mad bull.He chased them down with a knife - I begged him not to do it... but... he killed our children." She sank to her knees in anguish, words muffled by the hands that covered her face. "Then I cut my throat." Kath gasped at the stark finality of her words. Grisela smiled bitterly, "*Si*. I had nothing to live for...My son..." Her voice broke as Kath sank to the floor, cradling her in her arms.

"Shhhh...it's okay Grisela. You're safe now, he can never touch you here. I'll send for your things so you don't ever have to go back. No, I insist." She was firm and in charge now, armed with a mission, and reaching for the telephone.

Grisela watched her from the floor where she still lay, crumpled in a heap. She crossed herself twice rapidly, hidden by the mass of curly hair that now hung over her face like a dark web. The lie had been a big but necessary one. She knew from experience that few people if any, actually believed that such a hideous looking scar was nothing more than a birthmark. They actually preferred to think that she was a former gang member or worse. Her Mother used to say that sometimes a lie was more palatable than the truth, and she had been right, as always. She glanced around the room with its paintings and expensive furniture and smiled on the inside. She was going to love it here.

{4}

The Perfect Girl

Emme had the perfect figure – small waist, cute face. Like the kids said, a size four that could be a size six in the right places, if you understood how these things worked. Perfect skin tone too - not blindingly 'high yellow' but chocolaty velvety brown, so that when the light danced off it at some angles, she almost looked like a black Barbie doll. She even had the 'perfect' size foot: 7, or "sample size," as her fashion savvy friend Aliciaalways moaned to Emme enviously, whining about how unfair it was that she could never wear any of the Louboutins and Jimmy Choos that she had access to as perks of her fashion editor job. Instead Alicia had to gift them over to Emme, as she was the only one she knew well enough and *liked* enough, who had such narrow, "fairy feet," as she called them. But it worked out actually, because Emme always made sure to buy Alicia a corresponding pair in *her* size. She just was not the kind of person to accept such lavish gifts, especially since she knew that Alicia could offload those babies for a pretty penny on eBay (some Asian lady with loads of money and dainty feet would pay top dollar for them).Plus, Emme could afford it. Yes, the perfect girl also had the perfect job - go figure. Her dream job, for that matter, as a photo-journalist for a travel magazine.She felt extremely blessed to be able to get paid to do the two things she loved the most in this world – travel and taking pictures - and for good money, too.

Yeah, everything was pretty perfect for Emme. Now, if only she could find the perfect man to settle down with and have the perfect family, then this whole thing would be wrapped up. "Well, if *you* can't find you a man, the rest of us better call it a day," Yvonne guffawed at her own joke, taking a swig from her Michelob Lite. Raucous laughter followed, they were at their biweekly girls' time dates as they called it. Monica, the card carrying feminist of the group, had come up with the whole 'dating yourself' idea, which had been every bit as pathetic as it sounded, so it had morphed into them 'dating' each other – which wasn't nearly as weird or 'lesbianish' as it sounded. It was girl's night out with a little something extra thrown in, like little gifts for each other, or a spa party, or the hostess cooking or catering for the group. Tonight was just 'drink beer and build each other up' night. "Girl, can't nobody get a man for shit in this town." Emme concurred, "Except maybe Genna." Eye rolls and sputters all around the room. Genna was the only one in the group that actually did have a man and once she'd hooked her man, she'd been AWOL quite a bit except for when he was working. Like tonight. So she was fair game, and quite prepared to be hated on and butts of all the jokes. "See, y'all ain't right,'" she tossed her hair. "Maybe it's cos y'all hatin' bitches be hanging around each other," she said, her voice thick with exaggerated Ebonics (even more annoying as Genna was white, but considered the fact that she was dating a black man her 'pass') while deftly dodging a pillow tossed at her head. "You know like how women's cycles are in sync, sometimes?" A shoe narrowly missed her shin. " Let me even call my boo," at which time she was mock tackled by Karin.

"Well, I know why I can't get a man," Monica said decidedly. "I'm independent, strong, intelligent..." The rest of the women groaned in unison. "And we are?" Karin asked pointedly, mock offended. "Not." Monica continued, not breaking her stride. "So, as I was saying..."

"Ouch," Emme smiled, wryly. "Now, if we weak-minded, unintelligent, door-mattish, wimpy sorts can't find a man, that right there pretty much blows your theory out of the water, Einstein."

"This is true." Monica frowned, looking almost puzzled; now it was her turn to get mock tackled. "But seriously though, why can't Emme get a man? She's perfect. No homo, girl." They all laughed as Emme squirmed uncomfortably in her seat. These things usually turned into gossip-fests, where they picked each other apart in a sisterly, totally non-malicious way, of course. Of course. Coincidentally, they chose someone who wasn't there, or at least waited until the end of the night when they could blame their loose lips on the alcohol. *My bad, girl, those martinis are the devil! You know I can't handle my liquor!* Emme usually could take the ribbing, but she was just over it today.

"That's my cue, ladies." She downed her now warm glass of wine, picked up her clutch and stood up, holding up two fingers. "Deuces."

"*Awww...*"

"*Don't go! Come on, Emme!*"

"*You know we freakin' love you, it's just that you're so freakin' gorg, we just don't get it...*"

"*Men are sooo dumb, I swear!*"

"*Can I still borrow your shoes, though? Emme?*"

"*Gosh, we're such bitches...*"

Emme had to smile at that apt summation and retorted, "Make that *drunk heifer* bitches. Still love you guys, though!" And she did, but could only take them all together like that in extremely small doses, especially when they were liquored up.

She got into her Audi and felt herself relax. She realized that she'd been clenching her jaw and tensing her body a little bit in there. Whew, those biddies were really getting to her more than she cared to admit. They almost made her feel guilty for not having a man, even though they were all in the same boat. There was a lot of "but you're pretty... fun... have a great job... you're not a raving lunatic like me..." Well-meaning compliments that all served to make her feel even more inadequate. If she was so blessed and equipped with all the tools to get a man and still had none, then there must be something she wasn't doing, or worse, something wrong with her, like she was defective in some way. Her own mother had even insinuated that she was "lazy." Or was it "complacent." Same difference, it was still damning with faint praise. "I gave you the good genes, but I can't find you no man, now." And the 'picky' thing. Yeah, she'd heard that one to death, and quite honestly, she didn't hate it. At least, she wasn't being perceived as desperate enough to just settle. Well, she had pared her list down considerably as the decades rolled around, but it was not brought about by a sense of urgency: rather, it was more of a maturity thing, where the emphasis on the physical (height and skin tone specifics) was diminished, and the age bracket had been adjusted to her tastes. She was no longer averse to the idea of her potential mate having a kid or two; just the multiple 'baby mama' thing was still non-negotiable for her. As well as the no criminal records - she could sympathize. but was unwilling to be a player in whatever pathos that could ensue. Education and refinement was still a biggie for her; a lot of blue collar brothers made good money and were pretty refined, but she wasn't just into it. So, reasonable compatibility, a decent job and similar values was all she was asking for at this point and people talked about her like she needed Apollo's head on a golden platter. Was it really too much to ask for a dude to have a job, go to church sometimes, and not be an ex-con? She didn't think so. Matter of fact, her list was as bare-bones as it got. So then what was wrong with her? Or what was wrong with men these days? Scratch that - where were all the men though? Prison? She smirked to herself and shrugged off her inner 'Melissa.'

*** *** ***

She was home at last and thankful for it. Kicking off her pumps, she made a bee-line for her

Keurig coffee to sober up a bit, a quick shower, then her laptop, and bed. Nursing the dregs of her latte, she turned on her Mac and browsed her usual dating sites: 'Date-Match' was for hook-ups they said, 'E-harmony' for relationships, 'Black People Meet' for - well, black people, no? She'd finally figured it out, or rather admitted to herself the truth – it wasn't about her wanting the perfect man, it was that she *wanted* to *want* the perfect man.

But there was this new website she'd stumbled upon - bespoke.com. She hesitated a bit, like she always did, before she clicked on its shiny lowercase 'b' icon that she'd saved to her desktop. Maybe because it was just so *perfect*, and so *her*, she was a little afraid that it could turn out to be some cruel joke and disappear in a poof one day when she attempted to access it.

Bespoke ~ Be You. Everyone else is taken.

"Welcome back, Emme." A genderless voice greeted her and she felt instant release and a real guilty pleasure. Who knew that there were people *like* her out there? God knows, before she's stumbled upon the website a few months ago, she hadn't. One night after another frustrating 'non-experience' date, she'd googled 'uninterested in men or women' on a whim, and the word 'asexual' had popped up a thousand times over. She was familiar with the word, of course, but had just never thought of herself as being that. It just sounded so *sterile* and *plant*-like. 'Asexual living' had popped up. And so had 'association of asexuals' and 'asexuality in a hyper sexual world,' and tons of asexual this, asexual that. Okay, I get it, I'm asexual, she'd thought to herself, first with slight embarrassment and later with great relief. There was a label for people like her, she *had* people - she was odd maybe, but not alone. She'd read about people, mostly men it seemed, as being asexual, but it always seemed to be used as a pseudonym for being gay or somewhat less *than*. If a guy didn't desire his wife sexually, or other females, then of course he was gay, right? And she'd always imagined asexual people to be clinical almost, incapable of passion or romance, but she wasn't *that* way and she bucked against the very notion of it. She certainly wanted romance and was capable of loving and feeling and maybe even passion - she just hadn't met the right person yet.

She remembered college and her intensely promiscuous phase, chasing the elusive 'O' that her girlfriends so often gushed about. And she had boasted along with them, but meanwhile she'd never felt shit. That's when she'd realized it was all a big crock and orgasms existed solely in the minds of girls who wanted to please their men. And perhaps in the world of porn stars.

And there had been that time in high school when she'd cut her hair, found herself a girlfriend, and proclaimed herself a lesbian. For about a day. She had loved the softness of her lover's breasts and buttocks, yes. But truth be told, it was more about the aesthetic and texture, if that made any sense, than any real desire. And the 'o' had remained elusive.

So sophomore year in college, she'd stopped chasing it and stopped dating almost entirely and she hadn't even missed the part where you got to be with someone, she only felt lonely when everyone else was out on their dates. But she'd never shared this with anyone – gosh, no. She'd invented a few dates to keep everyone happy, gone on a few for real here and there, just *knowing* that nothing was going to come of them. And nothing ever did.

Until now - until bespoke.com, where she was amazed at the thousands of people out there like her. No expectations, just *being*. The mutual understanding and acceptance of no expectations was such a relief that she could literally cry. And now, everyone won. She would present an aesthetically acceptable, suitably *credentialed* man who made a decent living and had gone to all the right schools and her mom and friends would be happy. His parents and friends would be happy. She would be happy, he would be happy. The dating charade would evolve into a marital one and years down the road if they chose to go their separate ways, at least it would be on record that she'd tried. It would no longer be, "Now why can't Emme find a man? What's wrong with her?" It would go more like, "Yeah, he's a fool, leaving a woman like Emme, man." Or even, "You know how some of the finest women can't seem to keep a man? Emme on that Halle Berry *ish*." Yeah, she'd take even that, rather than the truth.

That she was perfect – perfectly *fine*, just not by their standards.

{5}

The Daughter

It was one of those days when the daughter was in what her mother liked to call her 'cruel and unusual ' mood, a play on one of the more commonly proffered reasons for divorce. The mother could always tell just by the way the daughter dressed that she was in a foul mood. The daughter didn't realize it, but she always actually looked the part - angry and unyielding - her hair pulled back in a tight bun, with her unflattering glasses (as she lacked the time and inclination for contact lenses when she 'wanted to bitch,' as she put it), and the monochromatic turtleneck and slacks. Always. Today she wore dark purple, complemented by the scowl that was so her father's.

"Don't judge me," the mother said, half-joking, as her daughter walked in the door, kicking off her Birkenstocks in one fluid motion, in readiness for battle. "Ma," a twist of the lips, she hated to be preempted. "That's not fair. I just friggin' walked in the friggin' door, who's passing judgments now, huh?" The daughter walked to the bar, still mumbling under her breath about the mother never having any *friggin'* drinks in the *friggin'* house.

The mother took a deep breath; she would try and be patient, try to ride out the storm. "I know a sailor raised you, but you will not swear in my house, got it? And next time, bring your own goddamned drinks." She bit her lips, holding back a chuckle at the daughter's almost chagrined expression. The mother hardly ever swore, and it was almost comical that she did so in the same breath while chastising the daughter.

"Ma, I don't want to fight." This meant, of course, that the daughter did. "But I think we need to talk about what Daddy did to you – to *us*. If you don't face it, we can never move on." She gripped the stem of her drink so tightly, the mother feared it would break into a million fragments, tiny glass shards becoming embedded in the thick carpeting.

The mother cocked her eyebrow at that. "We? I love how your father and my business has somehow become about you."

"It's always about me, Ma, you know that." The daughter's attempt at humor fizzled under the mother's withering stare.

"I just feel that you're in denial. That man never respected you, because you never felt you deserved respect. Sure, he brought you over here from Nigeria, but you paid him back, Ma. Don't you get it? You raised his children and worked as a nurse all those years, and that is enough!"

"Thank you for validating me. Looking at your behavior today though, I'm not so sure I did right by you." The mother was hurt now, she could feel the tears welling beneath the surface. It was altogether too much, too soon, this reliving of her past and reckoning with her future all at once. It had been decades, but some days, like now, the mother felt like she was still that young and bewildered girl who had travelled hours to a strange land to meet a husband she barely knew and be immersed in a culture she found bewildering.

"And how are you any different from your father? You don't respect me either; you never have. So how dare you judge him?" A more sensitive person would have sensed her hurt, which was palpable, barely hidden beneath the surface. The daughter, of course, was oblivious.

"And she defends him again." The daughter smacked her head in disgust. "What did he have to do to you to get you to admit that he wronged you? That man cheated on you from day one." She paused at the look of deep hurt on the mother's face. "I'm sorry Ma, but it's true and we all knew it. That man -"

"That man put you through private school, paid for all your hobbies and silly whims." She knew that would sting, the reference to the daughters artistic vocation, which neither of her parents had supported nor understood. "And your extravagant wedding..."

"That's what fathers do, Ma!"

"So he was your father after all, I thought he was 'that man'?" The daughter knew that the mother was really mad now, she had reverted to her native Nigerian accent, saying 'fada' instead of the softer, Americanized 'ther' with the refined 'r'. "I just don't understand how my acknowledging your father's..." the mother groped for the appropriate word, "...*indiscretions* could make you feel any better."

The daughter looked at the mother with something akin to pity. "Ma," her tone was gentle and patient, like she was speaking to a very old, senile relative. "Did it ever occur to you that maybe, just maybe, if you had shown me that you were strong and could stand up for yourself, I wouldn't be this way?"

"What way?" Even as the mother asked, she knew the answer, and she knew that the daughter knew that she knew, for they had been here many times before.

"I wouldn't be so angry, or feel I had to fight for you all the time."

"Is that what you call this?" The mother was almost amused now, "Fighting for me? It feels more like I need someone to fight *you* for me."

"I need to know that you know that it's not okay to just sit back and take stuff because some man - okay, your husband or whatever - dishes it out."

The mother knew that the daughter had always been a fighter. She had come out of her womb fighting, premature and covered with vernix, struggling to breathe yet squalling angrily. And years down the road, the mother had watched the daughter helplessly, as she fought these battles, real and imagined, some costing her great opportunities, friendships and more recently, a good marriage and a good man. The daughter was angry and the mother knew that her anger and fighting would not bring the liberation she sought. She had tried unsuccessfully to tell the daughter this, but the mother knew that this was not the time to reiterate this advice. Instead she said, "You need no such thing, daughter of mine." The daughter had turned her back to her mother and stood facing the wall on which the father's picture hung. "No matter what you think, he was a good man, your father."

The daughter turned to face her mother. "No, you are a good woman. He, on the other hand, was a liar and a bully."

"He is dead,child. Let it go." The daughter stood still, fighting back tears, determined not to cry for the father since she hated him almost as much as she loved him.

"Come, sit." The mother said gently, patting her lap. She laughed at the daughter's look of incredulity. "I know, you are not nine anymore, but you are still my daughter, are you not?' The mother pulled the reluctant daughter onto her lap and held her by her waist, half burying her face into her daughter's back, so that her words were muffled a bit.

"I met her, you know." The mother knew that the daughter knew who she was referring to by the way she stiffened and tried to look over her shoulder at her mother. The mother held her firm, she could not let the daughter see the hurt in her eyes nor bear the pity she knew she would see in the daughter's eyes.

"She came to see me after he died. She called first, and I agreed to meet with her. I knew I had to know, had to see what the other woman looked like." The mother's laugh was dry but without bitterness. "I thought she would be Caucasian and highly educated, you know, everything that I am not." She shushed her daughter's half protest at her self-deprecation." She was Japanese, a small and neat-looking woman, could barely speak any English. He met her at the deli near his office where he had lunch sometimes. He'd been going there ten years or so before anything happened. Who knows what sparked it? But then again, does it even matter?" This time the mother chuckled for real. "So you see, it wasn't I that was lacking, it was him. Your father was lacking in moral character." It was freeing to finally say it out loud.

The mother stroked the daughter's back. "Do you hear that? It was him, your father, not me." They stayed like that for a long time, Mother wrapped around the daughter; but it was in truth the daughter who clung inwardly to the mother, the mother whom she now recognized as truly strong.

{6}

The Father

THE BOOK OF LESLIE

The letter smelled how she felt Africa would smell. Its envelope was brown and large, like some kind of dusty, waterproof khaki, and its edges had curled a little, wilted with the vagaries of travel across the ocean, weary with dirt. After she had peeled off the stamp for her co-worker's son's stamp collection—it was a pretty one of a child eating a mango, somehow meshed with a barely decipherable outline of Nigeria—she smelled it and was instantly transported back in time.

She was eight again and sitting in her Daddy's suitcase, or 'box' as he referred to it, burying her nose in his clothes, which even after months in America still smelled of his home, Nigeria. She covered herself with his undershirts (in Nigeria they called them "singlets ," he had told her), disrupting the neatly folded pile which kind of looked like rows of powdered white doughnuts. Secretly she was trying to transfer her smell onto his clothes, to leave her imprint on him so that he would not forget her when he saw his 'other daughter'. His 'other family'. The ones who got to live in Nigeria with him.

"Your sister's name is Mani." This was how our father first told me about you, Mani. It was his way, as you know—no preamble and certainly, no sugar-coating, ever. "I have a sister?" I sputtered in disbelief, half excited, half-dazed. Surely, I must be dreaming. Then why were my ears aflame and my chest pounding like it was going to burst?

"Yes," he said, calmly reaching under his pillow for his beloved, well-worn journal that he wrote in every day. He brought out a picture and handed it to me. The photo had been taken in one of those ghastly looking studios, reminiscent of a really low-budget movie set. The girl in the picture stood ramrod straight and stared straight ahead in an eerie, semi-robotic manner, as if afraid to blink, or indeed, breathe. Her hair was held in two pony tails with gigantic baubles, and I remember thinking that she looked a bit like Minnie Mouse with her hair like that. It was hard to tell from the black and white picture what color her dress was, but it appeared starched, stiff and ruffled. It was her eyes that grabbed my attention though. They were our father's eyes—big, dark, thick lashed, arresting eyes. And she had his cocoa brown skin too, not like my fair skin that burned instead of tanning in the sun.

"Is she mommy's daughter, too?" Even as I asked the question, I knew the answer, but I needed to speak, to say anything to clear the sob that was rising up in my throat. Our father fought back a tiny smile. "No, she has her own mother, Leslie." He let me study your picture a little longer, the two of us sitting side by side in silence, before he gently raised my head up and cradled my face in his hands. "Ask me anything." I looked down at my hands and cracked my knuckles, trying not to look at our father, the center of my universe, this man whom I adored, who was telling me in this matter of fact way that there was another ME in another part of the world. In Africa.

"Why didn't mommy tell me?" What I really wanted to know, but lacked the nerve to ask was, why didn't *he* tell me? But I loved him so much, and saw him so infrequently that I could not, would not, risk making him mad, having him walk away. So subconsciously, I transferred the blame to my mother. And this would set the tone for our entire relationship through the years. She was there for me every day and thus taken for granted. My father, on the other hand, was not, and so he became this romantic, idolized figure.

"That, you must ask your Mother." He was standing now, hands in his pockets, almost jauntily. It was obvious that a weight had been lifted from his shoulders. He had told me his feelings and there had been no meltdown. The conversation was over as far as he was concerned; any residual resentment would be handled by my mother. And even then, as young as I was, and in spite of my inner turmoil, I was proud that I had not burdened him with the knowledge of how badly I was shaken, how hurt I was by his bombshell. Due to my maturity, he would not leave us hastily, and when he did leave, he would return quickly.

Dear Mani:

It is midnight-ish and the husband is snoring—rhythmic paced vibrations that serve as my very own white noise—which oddly enough provides me with the peace and quiet I need to read - no savor - your letter.

It was waiting for me like a prize, your letter, half propped on top of all the other magazines, junk mail, bills and what not. Of course, the husband did not sort through the mail like I would have done, even though he got home before- me. That, along with taking out the trash, and wiping down the toilet seat sprayed with his own urine, mind, are clearly beyond his comprehension. But I do remember, I promised not to overburden you with our 'old married couple' gripes anymore. Your point that some women would trade places with me in a heartbeat was well taken, and I am suitably chastised and repentant.

The Father

It really isn't as bad as I make it seem sometimes. If people were more honest, everyone would know that this is kinda what marriage is. Greg and I have reached a point in our relationship where almost all the kinks have been worked out—the sex is regular, if not earth-shatteringly great, the communication is as good as it will ever be, I think, and we have both learned to scrupulously avoid the things that drive each other crazy. It might be a dull marriage, but at least it is an enduring one. But for the fact that I, with my notoriously poor timing, have chosen to suddenly 'find myself.' Sigh.

Yup, I am finally doing it – I signed up for that writing class. I know this pales in comparison to your choices, or rather the freedom which you choose – like when you quit your great paying bank job just like that and fearlessly pursued your business venture. 'Buying and selling,' you called it, until you had gathered up enough capital to transition into what you really wanted to do, public relations and advertising. And I tell you, sister, although I am positive that you are great at everything you put your mind to do, this gig was MADE for you.

I can just see you now, with your three or four cell phones, clad in some terribly expensive, maybe even terribly inappropriate for work outfit, that you somehow manage to pull off. What is that phrase you always say? "There is nothing a Chanel boucle jacket can't dress up." See? I do pay attention to your ludicrous aphorisms. And I will save that one for the day when I actually can afford one of those bad boys and won't look a damn fool in it. But wait, I'm doing it again, aren't I? Gushing over you, and putting myself down at the same time.

I sometimes blithely refer to our father as the first man to break my heart, and although I joke about it, deep within me, I know it is in some way true. The complex nature of our father-daughter dynamic definitely laid the foundation of how I interacted with men later on in life. Several times, I've found myself playing the very role that I resent so much; of the passive woman who looks the other way while the love of her life waltzes between continents like some long-distance lover butterfly. Damn you, Daddy. I kid. I guess. Thoughts? Please, oh please let's 'Daddy bash' this once. It feels so exhilarating! Smiley face.

Good night, Sister.

*** *** ***

THE BOOK OF MANI

The phone rang just as she clicked 'send'. "Great," she muttered to herself. "What now?" as she leaned over to grab the phone and swivel over to her 'phone spot,' a little nook with a long bay window that overlooked the lagoon.

"This is Mani." There was no trace of any irritation in her voice, and her cryptic speech was softened by her low, smoky voice, efficient and professional, yet without being too 'receptionist perky'.

"Of course it's Mani. I bloody called you, didn't I?" The voice on the other end was Peter's, doing an over-exaggerated British accent.

"Mr. Odukoya, wonderful to hear from you," Mani said, a slight smile tugging at the corner of her lips, perfectly glossed in a becoming shade of coral.

"Yeah, it is, isn't it? I'm a pretty wonderful fella, they tell me..." His voice was teasing, a flirtatious phone caress. She felt herself getting warm as she crossed the room swiftly to shut the door. "How you dey?" she asked, reverting to the more familiar pidgin English.

"Like I no dey," came his flippant reply "I've missed you, Mani." He was serious now, the earnest Peter that she found so endearing, all traces of the privileged playboy gone. "It's been ages..."

She laughed out loud at that one, throwing her head back, enjoying the deliciousness of being desired by one you in turn desired. "Yeah, I guess three days is ages in 'Peterland', huh? Mister 'I-want-what-I-want-when-I-want-it'!" He laughed along with her. "You better believe it. Okay, so I'm hot for you, how we wan do am?" His tone was appropriately jocular, as befitting a 'friend's' husband, but it still couldn't mask the sexual tension between them. *I'm hot for you too*, she thought to herself silently.

"Abeg oh–more like you're hot for Toma oil," she chided him in a 'don't go there, I'm friends with your heavily pregnant wife' kinda way. But she made sure the undertones of flirtation were not completely erased, partly because, well, that was their thing – harmless and light. Denoting it as more would make things unnecessarily awkward, and truth be told, they both enjoyed their little banter. Besides, she rather liked Peter. *So sue me*, she thought, rolling her eyes at her inner moral compass.

"Well, that too. Now that you bring it up, where are we on that?" Peter was all business now, the positioning and branding of his oil servicing company, Toma Oil, once again his primary focus.

Mani switched gears along with him and scooted back to her desk, fingers flying over the keys of her laptop. "You've got mail, Peter. I think you'll be pleased."

"That's why I pay you the big bucks, Mani." The affectionate caress in his voice was back. Mani suddenly remembered the half-finished letter she was writing to her sister, Leslie.

"So, email me with your comments when you've had a look-see, okay? Gotta go, love."

"I'll call you tomorrow. Bye." Click. She smiled at the mild irritation in his tone. He so hated being dismissed, and this was another one of their little games; who would get off the phone first. Even if the person would find an excuse to call right back.

Yawning, she gave a faint sigh and shrugged her shoulders, while glancing at her slim Piaget watch in one fluid motion. Seven-thirty at night – no sense in trying to leave the island at this hour,– traffic would be madness. Best get back to letter writing. She gazed longingly at the laptop on her desk. It would be so much easier just to send an email, but she and Leslie had decided after a few attempts that 'Lols' and 'OMGs' just wouldn't cut it. Just about everything got lost in translation, and absolutely nothing felt as good as getting that envelope every week or so and reading Leslie's cursive writing, complete with the smiley faces and doodling that almost always accompanied her letters.

She and Leslie had received the news about each other in extremely different ways. First off, she and her siblings hadn't had the luxury of a heart to heart chat, or any formal chat from a parent at all. Instead the news had come from one of Mama's extra gossipy friends, who 'accidentally' let on in a roundabout way. When Mani had borrowed a toy, Mrs. Ajibade had come to their house, lips pursed and arms akimbo, muttering something about how her child didn't have the luxury of '*oyibo* half siblings to send her toys'. And it had all made sense then: Papa's frequent absences that Mama never seemed happy about, and the reason why they never went to the airport to pick him up, even though Mani would have *killed* to go; the hand-me-downs that Mama sniffed at but she and her siblings were grateful for; the muffled crying that she sometimes heard from her mother's room.

Mani wasn't resentful though. She was overjoyed to have a sister that was half American, half white. That made her practically American, herself—or so she told her best friend in school.

"When I'm sixteen, I'll go abroad and live with my sister, Leslie."

"Really?" Her friend Jowa was skeptical, and not a little jealous. "What if her mother doesn't like you?"

"She will," Mani said, with a little less certainty, "Or we will run away together."

"Hm, in the snow? You will freeze, oh!" They giggled together at the thought of Mani running in white fluffy snow.

They hadn't corresponded until their Father had died and Leslie had reached out tentatively. Her Mother had passed away years before, and suddenly, she was 'alone in the world' and 'freaked out'.

"You're hardly alone, Leslie," Mani had been amused at her dramatics. "You have five half siblings and my mother—we're yours, if you'll have us." They had all bonded in the month she had spent in Nigeria. Even Mani's mother, who had tried to maintain an icy reserve at first, had loosened up enough to give her a quick hug and sacks of fried groundnuts when she was leaving, enough to rival 'Planters peanuts', Leslie had said. But she and Mani had the closest bond. Maybe because they were the closest in age, barely six months apart.

Dear Sister,

It had started as a joke, this 'sister' thing, with Mani telling Leslie how if they'd been raised in the same household she would have been calling her 'sister' as a mark of respect. It had been a done deal for Leslie. "Sister it is," she'd said.

I must love you, I really must. I just cut short my conversation with the magnetic P.O to finish this letter. I know how you LIVE for tidbits from my incredibly glamorous life, so I must embellish heavily. Oh, the pressure! (LOL). But seriously, what are we doing, P.O and I? We could have dated way before he ever got married; Lord knows there was ample opportunity to. But nooo..., that would have been too easy—we are stubborn, block headed, complicated types, so we much prefer this wretched dance. Sigh. More fun this way, but gosh, I wish we'd at least attempted this 'thing' with a little more finesse. Because, let's face it, we are both driven, passionate people, perfect for each other in that way that could either be really good, or really bad. I'd have been willing to take that risk with him. Look at me getting all sentimental on you! But you owe me because I've been listening to you moan about your husband for years. So pull up a chair with a cuppa, it's gonna be a long one.

Ashi, P.O's wife, is, in the interest of full disclosure,my pseudo-friend. I don't know her all that well, but I get the feeling that if she was in the country more often, we would be girlfriends to some degree. In that 'let's go check out a movie with a bunch of other girl-friends' way, not 'let's hang out alone' way–gosh, no. Ashi is actually quite attractive, with dynamite legs, and from what I hear, a sparkling wit. I'd expect nothing less from P.O; a trophy wife just isn't his style, and let's face it, the man is too darned good looking to marry a dog. And now, Sister, she's having his baby; they are becoming this cohesive little family unit. And me, I'm still just a girl who likes a guy, that likes me too, but who also loves his wife and their unborn child. As it should be. I mean, I wish them well and would never try and jeopardize what they have; dating married men is not my style. But I kinda wish he was available because I am enjoying (and not exactly discouraging) this 'thing' with him, the flirtation, the open-ended chase where the pursuer is indistinguishable from the pursued. The deliciousness of this infinity ring of futility is almost enough for me. Almost.

THE BOOK OF LESLIE

Dear Mani,

Omigosh, the hubby actually checked the mail today! You laugh, but when you are married you quickly learn to pick your battles and rejoice in the little things, like mail pickups and clothes in the hamper instead of the floor.

I walked into class today, my stomach in knots, erupting butterflies. White button-down shirt, respectably dark denim, 'writer/nerdy' glasses carefully perched on top of head, securing my artfully messy bun; New MAC ensconced in artdecoish, pucciesquesleeve (on sale at Marshall's, thankyouverymuch!). Aspiring writer's exterior – check. Writers inner confidence, however? Double un-check.

What am I doing here? The class is such a writing class cliché, I can barely stand it. Of course, I'm contributing majorly to the situation with my perfect 'writer's ensemble', but come on! I look around me and I'm convinced for a second that it is all staged, a deliberate prancing exhibit? of wanna-be writers. There is a girl in a pink cheongsam and (I kid you not) slippers. yYour standard mix of writer 'extra' so and sos - people of all ethnicities and sexes with dress, turbans, holey jeans, harem pants and tunics. Every iteration of bangle, bracelet, piercing and tattoo is represented here in this wanna-be writers' puke-soup that I am now a part of.

Unnerved, I am just about to plot my exit when I hear a deep chuckle right next to me. "Scary, isn't it?" He is easy on the eyes, this one. "I mean, that we would have anything in common with anyone here." Coming from anyone else it would've seemed too familiar and a tad bit arrogant, but somehow, the way he said it, it worked.

"I'm Alex, by the way." his eyes crinkle nicely as he extends his hand. My belly does a little flip flop. Whoa. Easy girl. "Les." My voice sounds like it is coming from far away. Sister, I know trouble when I see it. Alex will be my kryptonite, I can tell— my Peter Odukoya. Now tell me sister, do we have Daddy issues or just slut issues? No, but seriously, we can blame our father for the former, but who do we blame for the latter? Ourselves? Our mothers? For what, pray tell? For loving a man that was 'unemotionally available', or rather, too readily available without discretion and discrimination, unbound by geography or moral code. Hm, this is some good stuff. Consider it copyrighted, haha. I love you, and I love the dysfunction that is us, but someone has got to break the cycle. Maybe a third sister in Asia? Jokes. But 'Papa was a rolling stone', so...

Night, Sister.

{7)

The Beggar

She would not take my money. I cannot fathom why it bothered me as much as it did, but it *did*. True, it was slightly embarrassing, but hardly the end of the world, as I have told myself over and over again. I will forever associate this encounter with the work of one prominent author I once read, titled, I think, "The Beggars Strike." The picture on the cover was of a hand stretched over a beggar's bowl, palm facing downwards. It had always seemed somber and chilling to me - why would a beggar refuse money, their very *raison d'être* for getting up in the morning?

I had seen her on several occasions in the winter, huddled on the other side of the streetin the covered alley, seeking refuge from the elements. She stood out from the rest of the 'street people' with her floor length fur coat and boatload of makeup, mostly red, so it looked as if she had stumbled upon a red crayon and scribbled on her face, or maybe fallen face forward into a bucket of red paint. I remember a guy turning to me one morning and remarking amusedly, "Well, isn't that something... begging for money and has the nerve to wear fur... probably has a house in the suburbs and an SUV... I tell you, these people, frauds every last one of them..." I didn't smile because for some reason I found his familiar approach a little annoying - he seemed to assume that I would share his views on pan-handlers. It was hypocritical of me, of course, as I was thinking the exact same thing; my 'holier-than-thou' attitude came solely from the fact that I was not forthright enough to voice my opinion out loud.

I grew bolder as the seasons changed, walking at an increasingly leisurely pace past her, making brief eye contact and gaining proximity. Why did I feel the need to work up courage to approach her and give her *my* money? I wish I could figure that one out. I did truly feel (even though there was absolutely no basis for this) like she was in a funny kind of way my secret friend, and that we were privy to an inside joke the rest of the world was excluded from. She was leaning by her usual bus stop post clad in old nurses' scrubs, sans requisite fur coat. Her lips were bright red as usual, but she had neglected to use her blush, or should I say rouge. I lingered around the general vicinity, pretending to be talking on my cell phone, while observing her through the corner of my eye. She looked like she might have come from money, or at least dallied with it, I thought. One could almost imagine her seated in some chauffeur driven luxury car, fur coat thrown carelessly on the seat next to her, puffing away on a cigarette with an elegant cigarette holder. For some reason, cigarette holders (circa 1800, I know) have always been the emblem of the absurdly rich and proper for me. While not pretty, you could tell that her face had been one that you would have looked at once. But age and hard street life had taken its toll, so she looked almost blurred now - like a smudged painting of a work perhaps titled 'The rich man's wife' or something along those lines.

"Can you spare a quarter?" I turned around, startled. It occurred to me that I had never heard her speak. In my head, I just knew that her voice would be throaty and rich, as if from smoking too many cigarettes and hosting the late night soirees that undoubtedly would have come with her status. Instead it was high pitched, nasal, and, I reluctantly conceded, annoying. She sounded like she was doing a bad imitation of some character — maybe Eliza Doolittle in 'My Fair Lady' minus the Cockney accent. Feeling disappointed and strangely sad, like she had somehow let me down by not sounding like I felt she would sound, I ventured close to her, fumbling in my wallet for a five dollar bill. As I walked towards her I noticed she had turned away from me and was looking in the other direction.

Determined, I turned around to face her, "Here you go..." I said cheerily, smiling and gesturing towards her cup. Her eyes - they were hazel - held mine for a second and I saw scorn, or was it disgust, and she slowly, deliberately put her palm over her cup and turned away. Stunned, I skulked away on wooden legs, praying that no one had seen me get rebuffed. (Again, why did I care?)

I could have sworn I heard her say, or maybe it was in my head, "I said a quarter, Bitch..."

{8}

The Dream

She'd had that dream again and had awoken in a cold sweat. She had been running, panting, chased by someone - or something. Not on foot, but a swooping equine-like presence – she sensed wings. How could she outrun it? Could a gazelle outrun an airplane? And to be honest, did she even want to? When she had turned around in her dream last night, she'd caught a glimpse of him - *it* - through her tangled web of hair and matted eyelashes, and he was beautiful, god-like almost, terrifyingly so.

She nurtured her dreams just as much as she feared them, and she was shamed by her secret longing for them, her panic when she did not dream. Once she had gone a week without dreaming and she had just about lost her mind.

She had bought lavender oil and bath salts, drank hot milk and googled 'how to make dreams', like an idiot. Where was he, it? Had he left her and gone to someone else? Someone more deserving, more attractive, more whatever? Just like her Daddy had left, and yes, her husband had left? There today and gone tomorrow, like poof! On an intellectual level she knew she was being absurd - dreams were just dreams. But she did feel a tad rejected, and yes, she knew she had daddy issues and abandonment issues, so there.

And then, just like that, one night she was in the forest clearing again. This time instead of running, she had steeled herself and waited. She wanted to see this one through. "It's just a dream, baby girl. You can wake up if you really want to," she told herself. But *could* she? Her stomach was literally in knots. Could he read her mind? She wasn't familiar with the rules in 'dreamland'. What if he thought she was taunting him and hurt her? Like, really hurt her, *Nightmare on Elm Street* kinda hurt. She shivered a little bit at the thought and also from the chill. Then it dawned on her that she was wearing very little – a silk nightgown was fine in bed, but didn't quite cut it in the forest. And the prickle on her skin was the kind you felt when someone was staring at you – you just sensed it.

And it – *he* - was. The most beautiful shade of blue-grey-green honey-flecked molten eyes were drinking her in. The way he looked at her took her breath away. It was like he was looking into her soul, and it made her want to weep and kiss him all at the same time. It was every kiss she'd ever known, every hug she had ever wanted, and all the perfect conversations she'd ever imagined rolled into one. And yet, it was just a look. She hadn't even noticed anything else before he spoke, but then she saw his lips were even more perfect than his eyes, if that were possible. And all she could think was, *"I hope this beautiful man-creature kisses me. Even if he is going to kill me, but please Lord, let him kiss me first."*

"That would be too easy," he said with a smile that made her want to dance for joy. He *could* read her mind (but of course!) and he'd answered her question almost before she'd asked it, it seemed. He wouldn't kiss her because he did not want to take advantage of her humanity, but yes, he wanted to and maybe he would. Soon. Her body tingled at the possibility. And just like that he was gone, just as he'd appeared, more a sensing than his physical presence, even though there was no denying *that*. But not before she saw his long hair and his gorgeous form, naked from the waist up, rippling muscles and perfect skin.

This time, she didn't awaken with a start, maybe because she had embraced her dreams and hadn't run. Who was she kidding? She hadn't wanted this to end. She felt like she had been rocked to sleep in her lover's arms. No, it couldn't be. She looked around, her room still looked the same, nothing out of order, no one had been in there. Sheesh, she'd definitely been without a date for far too long. Add that to her skipping her weekly therapy sessions for most of the year and her career as a romance novelist and she pretty much could write the script for what her therapist would say. Why even bother?

*** *** ***

"So tell me the part where you kissed the hot bird again." Her friend Trish was really beginning to irritate her. "He wasn't a bird!" she snapped. "Fine, bird-man or whatever. Sheesh, relax! I don't have a man, bird or beast, in my dreams or otherwise, so I am getting my rocks off vicariously through you," she batted her eye lids at Irene. "That's what us girlies do for each other." Irene had to laugh. Trish was a hoot, the way you could tell her practically anything and she would totally get into it, no matter how absurd, the way she referred to them as 'girlies', even though they were both well into their forties. Plus, she was hypersexual in a comical, school-girlish, romance novel type of way,so this was right up her alley. "How long was his hair - Fabio long? Cause eww!" They both laughed. Irene indulged Trish because let's face it, there really was no not indulging Trish and she did want to talk to someone, anyone, about the dreams. "Okay, for the last time, we didn't kiss – but we kind of did. With our minds." She felt stupid even saying it, but she needn't have worried on Trish's account. "Ooh, futuristic mind sex, hot!" Irene rolled her eyes, "It wasn't sex or kinky or *real* for that matter. But never mind, I'm about to be late messing with you." She left out the part where she had an appointment with a therapist – Trish was hyper enough as it was.

Once she got to the therapist's waiting room, she remembered why she hated therapists in general, hers in particular, and why she had stopped going altogether. It was all just so forced. The non-descript brownstone with hydrangeas planted in neat little bushes just so in front of them *see? I'm not for loony people, it's just tea at your best friend's house!* - forced beautiful. The waiting room was painted the perfect shade of ecru – how many consultations with the decorator had it taken she wondered? *Nothing jarring (might set the loonies off). Something gender-neutral (ALL loonies were to be made to feel equally welcome here). Definitely not white (too clinical - save that for the real loonies).* Ha! She was being unreasonable and petulant and she knew it, but *dammit,* she really hated coming here. She hated that she needed to come here, or rather she hated that all her life, people had told her that she needed therapy. Her mother, after Dad had left – why was *she* the one that needed the therapy? – her psych major boyfriend at the time, when her mother passed away. *You really should consider therapy, wasn't she like your only living parent or something?)* As if losing a parent was an illness and *not* going to therapy for it made her even sicker. Her husband – sorry, ex (asshole) husband. His therapy badgering had been the cruelest and the most incessant. It had started as somewhat of a joke. "You're nuts," he'd nuzzled into her neck one day, after a round of love making, "my nutty little peanut." And she'd rather liked it, at first – the 'little' and the 'peanut' part – it made her feel cute, protected and loved. These were of course, her Daddy issues surfacing - she did not need therapy to decode that one, but still she'd liked it. Whatever.

Then later he'd started to say it to her in anger, as an insult. The first time had been during an argument about something silly, a game of *Trivial Pursuit* or so, and he'd looked her in the eye and said coldly, harshly, "Nut job." She'd half laughed, certain he was joking, yet just as sure that he was not. "You are certifiable. You really should seek help for your 'episodes'," he'd continued evenly, unsmiling. And later, he had told her that he hadn't meant it, but she did know that she could be "a little crazy sometimes, right?" But he still found her adorable though, and he'd kissed her head in apology and she had never refuted it because she was his 'adorable crazy little peanut,' and if she wasn't that, then what was she?

The next time had been with friends at dinner. A friend that happened to be a nurse in a psych ward had mentioned how draining yet fulfilling her job could be, and her husband had said super casual-like, "Welcome to my world with this one." The silence that had followed was somehow louder than the awkward laughter that came seconds later, because he *had* to be joking, right? But he wasn't, and she sat there in her new jumpsuit, diamonds on her neck and tears in her throat, seething. When she had confronted him about it later, he'd laughed in her face. "For someone that's been in and out of therapy her whole life, you are awfully touchy. Maybe I shouldn't have said that at dinner, but all our friends know you're nuts. Lighten up, kiddo!" She had asked him how going to therapy for two periods in her life constituted in his mind "in and out of therapy," and he had been brusque with her. "Some people are more fragile than others, and that's okay. It's actually nothing to be ashamed of – matter of fact, I'll go with you."

That had completely thrown her off and disarmed her. Go to therapy with her? Well, if he thought it was a 'good thing' and wanted to do it, then why not go together? Never mind that before then it hadn't even occurred to her that there was any reason for her to go. But whatever, couple's counseling was never a bad thing, right?

The day of their first appointment, he'd been stuck in a meeting and so it had seemed perfectly logical when he'd urged her to go, since they'd paid for the session already. It would be a shame to waste it. "Besides, this is your chance to go tell the therapist how good you have it – and what a catch I am." He had teased her on the phone. She had glowed at that, and blushed and gone alone, because she loved him when he was being charming and nice to her. She had also been a little relieved that their couple's therapy had been postponed, because next to him she dimmed her personality so that he could shine, as the alternative was being diminished by him, his bullying, his nit-picking, his critiques.

Not surprisingly, he had never made it to a session, and gradually, she had even forgotten that that was how she'd started going. She continued because she enjoyed it, and it seemed he'd enjoyed *her* going. He was indulgent and understanding and would make remarks about how he "had his golf and the wife had her therapy and it kept them both sane." Or if she was stressed and raised her voice, he would ask if she'd been to therapy that week in the same tone a mother would ask a child if she'd taken her medicine. *Take your pills, crazy lady.*

But she was stronger than he thought; they were no longer married and she had gone to therapy for the divorce too, damn him. And now, with the dreams of bird-man, ha! She refused to go to her 'marriage therapist' - the wounds were still fresh and it really was time for a change. Plus this new therapist had had a cancellation, so it seemed like fate. A one time thing: divulge crazy, bird-man dream, be chided for having an over active imagination and for neglecting to go for regular therapy, get a prescription for her 'happy pill' and boom.   She'd be done with a check mark for completion.

The therapist, ("Nancy," she'd introduced herself with a smile) was not at all what she had been expecting and she'd seen plenty through the years. The aloof, all-business male ones that clearly should not have been counseling *anyone* about *anything*, let alone vulnerable teenagers like she had been. Devoid of empathy, worse than laboratory scientists, more like primatologists observing their animal of choice.   The slightly intimidating female ones who might as well have carried "I wish I had a penis" signs, because, well, they did.   They wore their femininity reluctantly and with resentment reminiscent of six year old boys in starchy shirts and bow ties. Their body language screamed, *"We are women but we can't change that - biology did that.   So to compensate, we will have walls full of plaques of degrees and other accomplishments and desks adorned with pictures of our pets and nieces and nephews, but none of our own children because we are workers first and maternal third or never. And our husbands or boyfriends whom we refer to as 'partners' understand this because they know we are equals in this journey through life together, and until they can have the babies, well... He is the Yale to my Harvard and we split everything down the middle because I probably make more, give or take a few thousands. Equality. Now what do you want to talk about today, young lady?" "Nothing," said her teenaged self in her mind. "Because we have nothing in common – I like boys, and I hated my mom for a lot of my life, but when she died, I cried. And I hated my Dad for leaving my mom and marrying again, but yet I miss him every day. So nothing. Because I hope to marry some day and have kids and call him my husband not just my 'partner'. And we have nothing in common, maybe not even a vagina."*

But this Nancy, she was different. First off, she actually looked like a 'Nancy,' like she would be at home in a country kitchen with a sizeable island and domed glass cake stands. There would be a red checkered cloth somewhere in that scenario too, and she would entertain and cut huge chunks of cake for her guests, in between puffs of some menthol cigarettes. Yeah, Irene was pretty sure there'd be cigarettes. But even the health freaks wouldn't mind, because it was Nancy, ya know? A solid, practical aunt that you could trust, good head on her shoulders but still human enough to make bad decisions like smoke and maybe eat too many pastries.

"So, tell me about him." Nancy sat back in her chair, with a smile and a definite twinkle in her eye. "Him? I don't -" Irene was taken aback by her direct approach, no preamble, no nothing. Besides, how did she know? Nancy's bosom and belly heaved with mirth at Irene's obvious confusion. "Or her. That person that brought you here today. It's always people, you know – our daddies, spouses, lovers, mothers, 'frenemies,' but someone is always at the root of our 'stuff,'" she gestured. "That's why I stick to animals myself." Another chuckle.

Stuff. She liked it. She liked the casual reference to her 'crazy' that made it less offensive without discounting it. And the 'our' was just golden. We *all* had *stuff,* right? You, me and even the country grandma therapist. "A birdman brought me here," Irene said softly, nervously, picking at an imaginary callous on her palm and waiting for the laughter she knew would come, especially from the less than stoic Nancy. There was no laughter. There was interest - but not in a teasing girlfriend way, not even in a therapist way - just pure, genuine curiosity. "Tell me about the bird man," Nancy prompted, "Where did you meet him?"

"In my dreams," Irene responded, "every night, for like, months now." And once she started she couldn't stop, the words tumbled from her, fast and furious. She tripped over them like rocks often, and only realized that she was crying when Nancy, wordlessly, handed her a box of tissues. Irene blew her nose, thinking to herself that she had to have exceeded her one hour session. She had spoken about her childhood, her parents, her ex-husband, the 'bird-man'. "So tell me, am I crazy? Or am I crazy?" She was being self-deprecating and bracing for the 'crazy stamp'.

"Of course you are," Nancy didn't miss a beat. "But aren't we all? That's why we have therapists.

That's why *therapists* have therapists." Irene couldn't be sure if Nancy was being irreverent or serious, but she didn't crack a smile. "I think the question you really want answered is what you should do about your birdman dreams. And my question to you is do you *want* to do anything about them?"

Irene took in some air, rife with indignation, "Well, I wouldn't be here if I didn't." Nancy observed her in silence for what seemed like a full minute and said, "Hm. Would you still feel this way if I told you that your dreams have nothing to do with your perceived psychological state?" Irene had to be truthful. "No."

"Well, then." Nancy was leaning back again, porch rocking chair style again. "Your dreams are just that – dreams. They don't make you crazy or not crazy. You are fixated on them for now because that is your thing. We all have a thing. I can prescribe you some really great sleep aids and that will pretty much take care of the dreams. But I do have a feeling that you might miss the – she made air quotes with her fingers - 'bird-man' interactions. I know I would." There was that sassy aunt again.

"So, I shouldn't worry?" Irene asked tremulously, in desperate need of reassurance backed by medical school and clinicals. "I wouldn't," Nancy said with a smile. "You're not off the hook yet, though – we still have Daddy issues and maybe a few ex-hubby issues to work through. Now therapy is not curative and there is nothing *to* cure. There are just things we need to manage. *Stuff.* Remember, we *all* have stuff." They hugged and Irene inhaled Nancy's scent of cinnamon and musk. She'd never hugged a therapist before, but then she'd never encountered one like Nancy before, either. Nancy winked encouragingly. "One more thing. You religious, by any chance?" Irene was a little taken aback by the question. "Um, I'm not *un*-religious – why?"

"Oh, I think you'll find this interesting. I 'dabble' in the Bible on occasion." She smiled cheekily as she scribbled on a post-it note and pressed it into Irene's hand. "Take care now. See you soon."

Nancy watched Irene leave with a wry smile and lay down on the couch that Irene had just been perched on. *Poor girl*, she thought, *her self esteem was in shreds.* She thought about the 'Nephilim" and how she could recite the verses by heart now. Irene's 'Bird-man'.

'The angels pulled from above and surveyed the beauty of the women on earth." *Genesis 6:1-5,* and 'The sons of God saw that the daughters of man were attractive..."

He would come to her tonight, Nancy thought to herself with a smile of satisfaction. She knew him well enough to anticipate when. And she welcomed it - it had been a while.

{9}

The Prostitute

The air was brisk and cold on his face that morning as he stood watching her walk away. It was ludicrous and he knew it, but he had to see her before the interview. *Had to*. She was his good luck charm, at least for this particular instance. If she had not propositioned him that night, he would not have thought of indulging in sex with hooker, not to mention on a crowded beach. They would not have felt starved after their almost feral love-making and would not have patronized one of the food vendors that sold their dubious wares by candlelight or lanterns, fish indistinguishable from meat, fried potatoes which upon tasting turned out to be yams. More importantly, she would not have asked for 'extra newspaper' to mop up the oily residue, grimacing like she was receiving sub-par service in a five star restaurant. And he knew he certainly would not have felt moved to wrap his shirt around her shoulders as they lay on the beach, the sound of the waves drowned out by the din of the live bands on the shore and the sounds of sex from the other working girls and their patrons. And they would not have had 'the conversation'.

"*Ashawo* no be work." He had started at the sound of her voice, throaty and matter of fact. As if it was the most natural thing in the world for them to be lying here on the sand, him shirtless and with her in his shirt and nothing else, smoking cigarettes and eating fried yam and fish. "So get a job then!" He wasn't sure what irritated him more, the attempt at conversation or the topic. It was a tad inappropriate he thought, to complain to one's customer about the tedium of the job while rendering services. "Ah...who wan give 'ashawo' job?" She laughed with real mirth. He shrugged in the darkness as if she could see him. She was right, but it irked him as he suddenly remembered why he had come to Bar Beach that late at night. He had no job, little money and no connections. He would smoke weed and fuck and eat until what little money he had was gone and then he would let the water surround him and it would be over.

"Where have you looked? You don check paper?" he said querulously, snatching the oil stained paper that held the remnants of their midnight feast.

"Ah no go school, who wan read am for me?" He held the paper above her head and began to read out fictitious job descriptions, as ridiculous as they were lewd. She laughed at his silliness and he laughed with her, enjoying her appreciation of his humor. He wasn't even sure how he saw the vacancy through the inky darkness of the night. It was one of those onsite interview deals, which meant they needed the position filled immediately - just show up with your resume, no torturous waiting period. It was definitely worth a shot.

*** *** ***

The beach looked different in the morning. The sand was littered with beer bottles, cigarettes and condoms, the remnants of the night that had not been washed into the water. She looked different too, but then again, so did he. He wore his best starched shirt and well shined shoes and she wore the same dress she had on the night before, except she wore it as a skirt with a simple button down shirt thrown on top of it. She had shrugged nonchalantly when he asked her if he could come back if he got the job, and had said something about the rates going up. She did not smile so he wasn't sure if she was joking or not.

He felt slightly irritated by her lack of emotion and general apathy. Had he imagined their camaraderie last night? Had it really been only about the money? He was annoyed with himself for caring, for coming here. He watched her until she was almost out of sight, 'dress-skirt' swaying in the wind.

She did not look back.

{10}

The Hawker

She felt the sun, hot against her ochre colored skin covered only by her flimsy t-shirt and the worn wrapper she wore firmly around her waist. She trudged wearily down the nearly deserted road, pausing to wipe the sweat that ran in small rivulets down her face. "Maybe I should just go home," she muttered to herself, looking to the left and the right before she crossed the road. The worst that could happen would be that Madam would beat her. She was no stranger to the whip; the lattice like scars on her back made that much obvious. It was the possibility of being sent back to the village to burden her ailing mother and many siblings that she could not afford to entertain.

Startled by footsteps coming in her direction, she spun around, steadying the tray of mangoes on her head with one arm. "Buy mango?" She eyed the man warily. One could never be too careful when hawking goods. Everybody had heard of the gullible girls who had followed men to remote locations to sell goods, never to be seen or heard from again. Not her, she vowed silently, and spat in the dust, watching him like a hawk. He stopped a foot or so away from her, pausing to reach into his breast pocket. He was sweaty, but neatly dressed in dark brown chinos and a blue shirt, the imprint of his singlet made visible by his perspiration. A bank teller probably, she thought as she sized him up, or maybe even a clerk in a law firm. He mopped his moist face rapidly, waging a personal jihad against the rays of sun. "Is this Herbert Macaulay road?" he asked. At her blank stare he assumed incorrectly that she spoke no English. He tried again, in pidgin. "Sister, dis na Herbert Macaulay road?". It was unfair of her, she knew, but she was irritated by this. Going by her humble attire of 'dunlop' slippers, worn t-shirt and wrapper, as well as her lack of response to his question, his assumption was perfectly logical. But she was irked by it all the same.

"I'm selling Mangoes, not giving directions."
She turned her back to him, a deliberate insult.
Stung by her sauciness, he jerked her, hard, by her
elbow from behind.

"Don't you touch me!" she yelped, jumping
into a tremulous karate-like stance, fear visible in
her eyes. At that he burst into laughter, broad
shoulders heaving and shaking. "Okay, okay," he
held up the hand with the handkerchief, waving it
like a white flag. "I won't touch you again. But tell
me, why are you so prickly?" His eyes, nice and
kind, smiled along with his lips. "Me, I just want to
sell my Madam's mangoes, that's all." Her words
came fast and furious, and she was suddenly
embarrassed at her disproportionate reaction.
"Hmm," his eyes were still twinkling as he looked at
her, stroking his chin in a deliberate, playful
manner. "So what is Miss Mango Seller's name?"
He was trying to be charming and she prayed her
flushed skin wouldn't display her pleasure at this
unexpected attention, as she hissed scornfully and
readjusted her tray on her head.

"Tell me your name and I'll buy a mango."

"Fifty Naira." She held her breath, waiting for the epithets that she anticipated would follow.

"Jesus of Mecca! For one little mango? Is Nigeria that bad? This damn inflation, eh?" She couldn't help smiling a little at his exaggerated reaction, especially when he scratched his head, as if truly perplexed.

"Twenty."

"Forty five Naira, last price."

"Fifteen Naira. The longer you haggle, the lower my offer gets." It was hard for her to tell if he was still teasing her, but she noticed that his eyes no longer twinkled. Her chin wobbled under the pressure of holding the tears in. Madam had told her not to come back if she didn't sell the entire tray of mangoes; it was already mid-afternoon and *zilch*.

"Please..."

"I hate phony tears even more than I despise thieving little street urchins..." Her lip quivered and she burned with shame at how he perceived her. "My madam will kill me..." she snuffled like a child and tried unsuccessfully to wipe her eyes, while balancing the tray on her head. He hesitated, expression softening, reaching out to steady her tray. "Here you go," he proffered a crisp twenty naira note in her direction. "This is the most expensive name I've ever had to purchase." He smiled when he saw her grin reluctantly through her tears. Her lashes were impossibly thick and dark, he thought to himself.

"My name is Rakia." She sat down at the edge of the ditch, watching him as he leaned his lean, long body against the bus stop pole. "Rakia." He rolled the name around on his tongue, savoring it. "So what does Rakia do when she is not selling mangoes?" *Easy man*, he thought to himself. He was flirting with this young, unexposed yet incredibly attractive hawker child and he was enjoying it immensely. She was momentarily tongue-tied. No one had ever really expressed an interest in who she was or what she did - surely it was obvious that she was hired help of some sort. "I serve my Madam..." she broke off and added hastily "...but I will go back to school next year. I want to get my High School Leaving Certificate." She wanted him to know that she was not the 'street urchin' he had so scornfully labeled her; she was a young woman with goals and ambition. He looked at her thoughtfully and said, "That's excellent Rakia, good for you." She felt hot all over as she saw him looking at her in that manner. They were silent for a couple of minutes, staring out onto the road. "So, is this Herbert Macaulay Road, or is that information worth another expensive Mango?" They smiled at each other, bound momentarily by their inside joke. "No, it's the next street on your left when you get to the T-junction." Her makeshift beads jingled as she gestured in the general direction.

"Good bye, Rakia." It was a light touch, more like a caress, to her elbow. She watched him until he turned the corner.

"Bye..."

She realized she did not know his name.

11

The Coma

The machines beeped and whirred all around the room. It was large by any hospital standards. She was to be given the best medical care money could buy. This was to be expected; after all, she was a Garba. Only the best for a Garba, of course. He would never actually say that though: he was way too polished, way too skilled and practiced at being the rich-yet modest, rich-yet humble, *rich-yet-not-new-money'-rich* Garba, to ever utter those words.

But his status was implied in all the unspoken details - the urgency of being 'med-evaced' from Nigeria to Switzerland, the request for the most secluded and luxurious room that was available—all explained in a 'hush-hush' tone hinting at the instability of Nigeria and how the disparity between the wealthy and not so wealthy made it unfortunately of the utmost importance that the staff be discreet. And of course the additional security at the door was completely necessary; there may or may not have been assassination attempts on members of his family in the past.

His wealth was implied in his fluent French and the common network of friends in Lausanne that he shared with the surgeon. Boarding schools and Swiss banks and charities that only the really, really rich cared about. And he would have the grieving husband routine down pat too. He would wear his grief like a well cut suit–with ease. No flashy colors or loud pinstripes–his only jewelry would be his watch, perhaps a Patek Phillipe, and his plain gold wedding band.

His grief would be understated and appropriate, tearless yet moving–the grief of an incredibly wealthy young man whose wife with whom he is besotted had fallen into a coma from which she might never awaken, or from which she could awaken tomorrow.

36 hours earlier

It had been a good day. She had just cleaned house emotionally and literally; 'clean floors, open heart' her mother always said. To the housemaids' chagrin, she had tied up her hair in a kerchief and started scrubbing the floors at six in the morning. She shooed them away with a smile–the first genuine one in months, it felt like. She and Hassan were finally in a good place, sort of. Tonight would be the deciding night though - were they getting back together? This was an odd question in itself, as they had never officially separated. Yet they had in a weird way: the separate bedrooms, dwindling nocturnal conjugal visits, more and more of her meals going uneaten by him, and no attempt at conversation that did not involve the family business. But they were getting back together, she smiled to herself knowingly - a woman just knew these things. He had been very romantic and contemplative in the past few days, exactly how he'd been before the proposal. She'd known then, and she knew now.

He'd had no idea that she'd chosen to get a French manicure the day before, just to set off the engagement solitaire that he had picked out guided by her BFF, who had been guided by her (yay for girlfriends!).

She had almost felt sorry for him back then, sweating bullets, the expensive Japanese food probably tasting like cardboard in his mouth- too cute.–But a little part of her had savored the moment in a way, for it would never be like this again. He would never desire or love her quite as much as he did at that particular moment. To hear her married girlfriends tell it, he'd never even come close to that feeling ever again. So she let him sweat it out, knowing that she looked absolutely amazing in her Kelly green cheongsam dress, knowing she would say 'yes.'

But of course! She was playing coy, not plain crazy. She truly had never loved anyone quite as much as she did him. He was smart, handsome, and being a Garba didn't hurt either. She was no gold digger, but as a realist she had to admit that marrying him would mean marrying well. Very,

very, very well, indeed. That she actually enjoyed his company was a nice bonus.

After the engagement, she'd gotten her first taste of the perks of being the soon-to-be Mrs. Hassan Garba—the business class trips, the chauffeurs and chefs, the five-star hotel weekday stays just because, and the front row tickets to all the hot shows.

She had never minded paying her own way before and was pretty much self-sufficient, but a girl could get used to this. And Hassan had loved showing her his world. He drank in her reaction like smooth, premium vodka, reveling in her wide eyes when he said a little too casually for the umpteenth time, "Yeah, we own that hotel, too."

"Do you own everything in this country?" He'd tapped her nose gently with his finger and said quietly and almost soberly, "Not yet, but we will." She was no green ingénue, but in the face of such wealth and power it was hard not to feel that way; it was impressive.

What had sold her though was the fact that she had never heard rumors about him and some side chick, as was the norm for the wealthier dudes in Nigeria. She expected it, dreaded it, but accepted that it was probably inevitable that he would cheat on her, but was very grateful that if it was going on, her face was never rubbed in it. The only cause she'd ever had to harbor any suspicions was that he was filthy rich, not bad looking, and well, he was after all, a man.

"Hey." He peeked around the pillar and stared at her in disbelief. "No wonder the servants are all atwitter." He laughed, "You are turning their universe upside down. When ladies of the manor start mopping floors, scullery maids have job security nightmares, you know?" She laughed with him. *Gosh*, it felt good to be here again – easy conversation, semi-flirtatious camaraderie.

"May I buy you a meal?" He was serious now.

"You got money, I got belly!" She winked at him. Yup, she was flirting with Mr. Hassan Garba– *her* husband!

"Great. Wear something nice. There might be a little accessory for you on your vanity." That boyish smile again and he walked away, whistling.

Her heart sang in cadence with his whistle. It was almost like he was courting her again— the teasing, dinner, the jewelry. She knew whatever he chose would be tasteful, beautiful and, well, expensive.

Her engagement ring had started the solitaire trend amongst their circle of friends - no gaudy cluster of diamonds set in bright, impossibly shiny 24 carats Saudi gold for her. Hassan had designed the most perfect, dazzling yet understated pink solitaire diamond set in a thin platinum filigreed band.

"There is only one like it in the country, maybe even in Africa," he'd told her, "just like you." And her heart had glowed. For each anniversary— they'd had three together thus far—she'd gotten a necklace, or some earrings, or a charm to add to her gorgeous bracelet that had been his wedding gift to her.

"I'll fill this thing up pretty quick; you might need two."

"How so?" she'd asked. She knew he liked to talk about his love for her and spoil her rotten, and she loved to listen to him, to let him love her.

"Oh, for our fourteen children we're going to have," he'd said with mock seriousness. "That's your duty as a Garba; it's in the fine print." She had playfully clobbered him with a pillow and they had laughed it off, but her laughter belied a niggling worry that that she had, perhaps the only real one. What if Hassan tired of her and chose to not only take a mistress but to marry her? It was not uncommon, even in their polished, Westernized elite circles. Some would say it was even worse, the swiftness with which the 'old wife' was replaced and ostracized, the way the phone calls stopped, the averted eyes. There were no whispers; there was dead silence which was way worse.–It was as if you never existed.

Sometimes the perks would remain if the husband was kind, but there were conditions to them, and a humiliation pervasive in one's continued acceptance of these 'perks,' as if you'd sold your birthright for spa treatments and airline miles. Most first wives went quietly into self-imposed exile - in another country, maybe, devoted themselves to a charity to create a whole new identity for themselves. Or it became all about the kid; the title was 'mother' now and not 'wife and mother,' but at least there was *a* title and an acknowledgment. Three years in, she had no kids and although Hassan swore it didn't bother him and that he was enjoying it just being the two of them, it really, really bugged her. Yes, there was no cause for alarm *yet*, but she felt silent pressure from her mother, from society, from her expectations of herself. There should be little Hassan Garbas running around. So lately when he became distant at first, then irritable, then both distant *and* irritable, she had known that what she feared the most had happened. He had tired of her and she didn't even have the security of at *least* being the mother of his children; at best, she would be the 'ex Mrs. Hassan Garba.'

"She cannot have children," they would whisper about her.

"Na fine face we go chop? We cannot eat beauty, *nau*!"

"What a pity," the self-righteous gossips would say. "These educated girls, only God knows what they do to their wombs in University, eh? With abortions, careless sex and what not."

She'd lived in hell for the greater part of the year, since he'd shut her out for no apparent reason. Like she had told her mother, how could she have a baby if he wouldn't touch her? Her mother had been uncharacteristically unsympathetic. "Then you must *make* him touch you, *haba*! Don't say this outside oh, that you cannot make your husband desire you?" Her mother dry spat. *Tufia*. "No one taught you the other things you know, no one will teach you this one, you hear?" There it was, the scarcely veiled insult and implication that she had been sexually precocious, from her own mother. But even as it smarted, she agreed with her mother. Hassan had desired her before; how could he not anymore? It was just that she had never been entirely sure that it was anything she had done or any particular quality that she possessed that had made him seek her out in the first place. How could she recreate something she never created in the first place? *He* had chosen her. She wasn't more attractive or interesting or harder to get or anything really more than all the other girls. She had been just as excited by him from the jump as everyone else had, so it was baffling. His love had been inexplicably bestowed upon her. And here they were reconnecting again now, and like before, she had no idea why or how.

In recent weeks, he had taken to staring at her wistfully when he thought she wasn't looking, and kissing her thoughtfully on her forehead like in the good old days. And now today, a dinner date. *Yes*! What would she wear? Best look at the 'accessory' he had got her first, and then work from there. As usual, his taste was impeccable - understated elegance with a 'wow' factor. It was hard to beat Hassan on taste, that was for sure. The diamond encrusted single stem orchid brooch would go perfectly with her high necked Donna Karan maxi sheath dress that she'd never worn before. The plunging 'vee' at the back more than made up for the modest front; the silk blend of the fabric skimmed her curves in a suggestive yet classy way. She was going wear the brooch on her bosom as her only adornment, but after she put her hair in a sleek chignon she decided to secure the bun with it instead, and wore a Lariat necklace down her back. Simple diamond studs, metallic Manolos, and she was ready to go.

Mrs. Hassan Garba was the luckiest woman in the world tonight, and the look in his eyes coupled with the firmness of his hand on the small of her back told her that he was feeling pretty lucky himself. "Brilliant, my dear," he muttered in her ear as he steered her towards the maître d'.

"Private room tonight, sir?" The maître d' was all bows, scraping and smiles;the Garba patronage was not to be taken lightly.

"No, not tonight, thank you Razzaq. Just a table for two, maybe an alcove on the upper level. Do you have any space up there?"

"For you, sir—always. Madame, if you will, this way please." She bestowed a charming 'Madame' smile on him - graceful nod, slight baring of teeth, not too approachable but not bitchy ice queen either.

He ordered for both of them, as usual, but meeting her eyes for confirmation that she'd have the duck with sauce on the side. not on top, and vegetables instead of the mashed potatoes.

"My wife is on a diet, but she has no need for it as you can see. Maybe she's trying to tell me something," he teased her and included the waiter at the same time, and they both glowed. Yes, he had that effect on people. She heard 'my wife' and knew that the champagne would be completely unnecessary, she was already high. He didn't talk much, just stole glances at her from time to time. She blushed with each glance she caught. She felt like they were back in the old days when she was daring to hope that she was enough, that regular old her could attract and sustain the interest of *the* Hassan Garba. Even after they had dated for a while, she never really believed they would get married. It wasn't an inferiority complex, it was just the way things were and she was a realist. Rich, eligible, big name Hausa men from certain families did not marry middle-class girls from the east. They did not marry for love—they married to cement relationships, build dynasties and repay debts. Marriage was a currency people like her just did not deal in and she had been fine with that. She decided from the jump that she wouldn't be bitter, but would look back on their dalliance in college fondly, and would marry an upwardly mobile man from her world and that would be that—no hard feelings. So when he had asked casually if she would mind meeting his folks, she had literally gasped.

"How do you mean?" she'd sputtered. He had been amused at that.

"Was that ambiguous? Unless you'd rather not meet the 'Malus'." He used the derogatory term for Hausas to put her at ease, because she had to admit, he made them 'Malus' look good. "Um. Sure. Yes, I-" He'd kissed her swiftly.

"Thank you. I think it's prudent to meet one's future in-laws at least once before the wedding." And later she had tried to recall if he'd said 'potential' or 'future' in-laws, but it was mind boggling to her that he had even alluded to the possibility. These things didn't happen to girls like her. She'd never even dated the popular guy in high school or college before him, and now she was dating and possibly marrying the guy.

"You're not talking much," he said. "Neither are you." She smiled at him shyly. "I'm stuffed." "Yes." He was thoughtful again. "Things have not been right between us for a long time." His voice was low and soft but she heard every word. Again her breath quickened.

"No."

"I want you to be happy. I can't make you happy—we cannot make each other happy." His words were coming fast and furious, almost in keeping with her breath. She felt faint, almost, and his voice was coming from far away it seemed. Was he-? It sounded like—was he breaking up with her? He was. *He was.*

"I want you to have everything you want. The house. The one in London too. Anything else you want – "

"Stop." She raised her hand to silence him. "I don't want anything." She did, but she wanted them together—more than houses, more than any real estate—yet her brain could not seem to send the signals to her mouth. Besides, her mouth felt so dry. Where was that wine again? "What are you saying?" she managed to croak out. She knew what he was saying; why in god's name did she need to hear him say it again? His eyes were moist but his voice was firm. "I am not-" he hesitated, "I am in love with someone else." Wait, *what*? She had been semi-prepared for him to have fallen out of love with her. Yes, the signs had been there, but this– her existing replacement–was like a sucker punch to the face. When? How? She had been pining away and scrubbing floors and somehow, he found time to date, to fall in love, to make divorce plans? She was caught off-guard; no, she was devastated. She raised a forkful of crème brûlée to her mouth and let it slide down her throat slowly; deliberately. It gave her something to do while she willed her brain to work, her mouth to formulate questions.

"Who is she?" Her tone was almost level, barely a tremor. Now his gaze faltered. "I think it best-"

"Who is she?" Her voice had raised half an octave louder. If he had thought that bringing her here to this fancy restaurant would be his buffer from a melodramatic meltdown then he had miscalculated gravely.

"It's not important." She gave him a look of hate and scorn.

"Only important enough to throw your marriage away."

"Let's not do this here." He was mad now, and spoke through gritted teeth.

"Too late for that." The angrier he got, it seemed, the calmer she became. "You suggested this place, remember? You brought me this- this brooch." She yanked it off, dislodging her chignon. She had started to throw it at him but he stopped her with an icy look and raised tone.

"Don't you dare."

"And why not?" she taunted. "The Garbas have a ton of money don't they? So how many of those baubles does you Mistress have?"

"She is not my-"

"Lies!" She put her palm in his face and watched him wither with embarrassment then shut down completely.

"I will not dignify your immaturity with the reaction that you are seeking. I'm done here." His tone was arctic.

"Well, I'm not." She was enjoying this immensely, his discomfort.

Oh, this would make the gossip rags this weekend for sure. The Garbas were obsessive about keeping their names, and even photographs, out of the media unless it was associated with business, charity work, or some other semi-philanthropic effort. Ever since the South African blood diamond rumors had all but shut down her father-in-law's presidential bid, they were under strict instructions from on high not to do any high-profile interviews, appearances, or anything, unless it could stand up to tough media scrutiny.

The waiter shifted uncomfortably, not sure what to do. He didn't want to make his top patron uncomfortable as he sensed there could be a disagreement. But to ignore Mrs. Hassan Garba's obvious agitation could be fatal to his tip. What if they were just having an animated discussion?

"Madam?" She ignored Hassan's glare of death and responded. "Ah, yes- I'll have some coffee and more of this delicious crème brûlée. Coffee for my husband; black please. She emphasized the 'my husband' just to piss Hassan off. The waiter bowed and practically skipped away, happy to be of service and out of the line of fire.

"What the hell are you doing? You're going to regret this you know."

"Is that a threat? Sounds like a threat to me." She caught the eye of someone at a table nearby who was trying and failing miserably not to look. "You're my witness," she raised her voice, "You are all my witnesses, if anything happens to me-" At that, Hassan sprang up, European boarding school niceties abandoned. He grabbed her arm and yanked her up. "I'm afraid my wife has had way too much to drink," he said to everyone and no one in particular; he couldn't meet anyone's eyes as he jostled her towards the spiral glass staircase. "Let's go home dear, so you can sleep it off." Now she was scared. His fingers were clamped on her elbow like a vice of steel, the threat in his voice was just as real. She'd never seen him angry–

like, never; not like this. She didn't know what to expect and *that* was scary. A sob caught in her throat, "*Please, Hassan, I'm sorry! Please...*" she began to scream and the last thing she remembered was thinking, "*I just want to know who she is, before I die, before he kills me.*"

*** *** ***

The headlines were brutal and the witnesses were even worse. Most people seemed to remember her being pushed down the stairs but the restaurant staff and management, predictably, said she might have caught her heel on the stairs *but this in no way was an admission of any liability on their part.* Had she been drunk? Had he pushed her? No one could say for sure, but it definitely looked bad. There had clearly been a fight. And the words 'mistress' and 'divorce' had been bandied about. *A lot.* The Hassan-Garbas weren't so high and mighty after all. "*Hm, men, eh? Too wicked, oh!*" The women clicked their tongues in pseudo-sympathy; they had not married into the elite, but they hadn't been pushed to their deaths, either. The men were just relieved it wasn't them or their families in the scandal section of the news. And there went any political ambitions he might have; even worse if she didn't make it. He could never be with his mistress *now*, at least not for a good while. What woman would want to be known as the one partially responsible for landing another in the hospital and possibly dead? Dating *anyone* for Hassan Garba would be totally out of the question as well; even if whomever he was seeing wasn't *her,* it sure would look that way, and no one, least of all Hassan himself had the stomach for the messiness of the entire situation. It looked bad from every angle, this coma.

So here she was, in the pristine, clinical world of beeping and whirring. In her comatose world, she could sense everything around her with no external expression. She had felt panicked at first; like she was submerged in water, drowning amongst lifeguards and swimmers. *Can't you all see me thrashing around? Save me!* She had given in soon enough, and she now quite enjoyed this secret, private world. She never got hungry or felt pain here. She was almost detached, like she was floating above her body. It was almost like attending one's own funeral. It was shocking how unguarded people were when they thought you were too sick to hear them. She was more up to date on the doctor's prognosis than her husband and concerned family were. Her chances of recovery were about thirty percent, but they told her husband fifty percent, because that is what her heart-broken husband would want—or so they thought. Besides, they could not risk him getting frustrated and moving her to another facility that promised a quicker recovery, so they would tell him, say, after about a month. Also, she could potentially wake up on her own; the human body was a wonderful, mysterious thing. It was amazing what one could will themselves to do *if* they wanted to.

"And I'm sure she's a fighter, *Monsieur* Garba?"

"Yes." His voice was soft and low; she could imagine the bitterness he must feel towards her right now. *Wake up, bitch.* Maybe she was being a little too harsh; he probably had never wanted it to come to this, but he would have to know that if it came to her willing herself to wake up, that was probably never going to happen.

"*Oui*. The human body is a very funny, mysterious thing; a lot of this medical stuff –is just *stuff*. We are the best healers of ourselves. She will wake up; of this I have no doubt. The when–we cannot say just yet; but it will be when *she* wants to wake up and not before." She had smiled inwardly when she heard that. She could almost see the slight tightening of his jaw; his darkening face. He would *never* leave her now. Standing up to his father would never happen–the Garba legacy trumped whatever passion/love/affair thingy he had going on with *whomever*.

She would stay here a while. Here she was *still* Mrs. Hassan Garba; Hassan was still ostensibly hers and hardly ever left her side. Yes, she *liked* it here.

12

The Widow

D id widowhood begin when they gave you the news that you were indeed a widow? Or did it start before that, from the very minute your spouse slumped and diedlike Igwe had, all Brooks Brother's suit and tie, manicured nails, but still very much dead, head toppled forward on his impressive, imported oak desk?

It had been hours before they had discovered him, as he had ordered his timid, green receptionist to hold all his calls; he was not to be bothered, under any circumstances. If a tree falls in a forest and no one is around, does it make a sound? If your husband dies and no one knows it yet, are you in that moment, a widow?

The Widow

The very instant Igwe had died she was probably getting her toes painted in a becoming shade of sea foam green - pastels were in this year.. She had only officially found out hours later though, while - even worse - having her hair washed.

"Madam," the girl had timidly handed her the buzzing handbag that housed her buzzing blackberry. "Your   phone dey ring."

"Thank you, my dear." *I've got to remember to tip her*, she thought to herself, the shampoo girl and stylist were always on her radar, but their receptionist slash 'girl Friday', she sometimes overlooked. She reached for her phone gingerly, her nails were probably dry, but one never knew. It would be Igwe, of course. He always wanted to know where she was, even though he was aware of her weekly Wednesday rituals. Massage, nails, hair, home in time for date night. Repeat again on Saturday, except substitute date night for something with the kids or entertaining friends. He liked her to look good and she did not mind being pampered, so it worked for them.

The number was an unfamiliar one, so mouthing an apologetic "no vex" to the shampoo girl, she walked towards the lobby, hair dripping, the lavender scented towel around her shoulders dampening rapidly. There was a voicemail. "Mrs. Iwunna, please call me back. I have some urgent news about your husband." Her stomach did that funny thing it did when she was going to be sick. And at that exact moment she *knew*. Igwe was dead. She tried desperately to grasp at appropriate scripture dwelling in the murky recesses of her mind. *We walk by faith and not by sight....* No *weapon fashioned against him....* Nothing seemed to fit in that moment. Then she tried prayers and solemn oaths. "God, please let him not be dead. I promise I'll never miss a day of church..." Then: *Don't do it for me, Lord, but please, please, please, do it for those children who need to see their Daddy tonight.*

She realized how she must look, a well-dressed lady in the middle of the room, with sodden hair and damp back, clutching a phone and muttering to herself. *Don't be a drama queen. You haven't even called the number, silly. Breathe,* she told herself - *don't bury him before he's actually dead, geez.* It seemed like the phone barely rang before she heard the voice on the other end. She didn't remember the delivery, but she remembered her screams and the pandemonium at the salon. And then, the nothingness.

The funeral hadn't been so bad, she thought to herself. It was the people, either they whispered or they spoke very loudly to her. Did people equate losing one's spouse with loss of hearing or being unduly sensitive to normal speaking voices? Oh, and the lack of sunlight. Every other phrase out of her mother and her mother-in-law's mouth had been 'draw the blinds, we are mourning." Igwe was shut up in a box under the earth, so his widow had to simulate the same. *His widow.* Yuck. Her gold wedding band winked treacherously at her, even in the dimness of her room. It had been on the tip of her tongue to ask just how long 'mourning' was, not because of any burning desire to go partying and such, but because the rites and rituals that came with widowhood were innumerable. Not to mention, exhausting.

She wouldn't dare, of course. Aside from wanting to honor Igwe's memory and all; he *had* been a good husband, provider, father and friend.

It had been tough the first month or so. She had insisted on sleeping in his shirts and on their bed, to her mother's chagrin. She'd drawn the line at her 'ladies in waiting' sleeping in the same room as her.

"I feel like I'm on suicide watch. If I can't have a few moments to be alone with my thoughts, I *will* kill myself, for real." *Or one of you,* she'd thought to herself. That had made them back off, but she was pretty sure someone had been designated to sleep outside her door. Just in case.

Even harder than that, had been telling the kids. Nneka was still too young to fully understand, but Ugo and Ike, preteens, had to hear it from her. Her heart broke as she watched them try to straighten up into what they thought was a more manly stance, their high voices negating their claims to instant maturity. And the thought that their only daughter would never really know her father, who had adored his daughter, made her crazy. "Your Daddy is in heaven." Did uttering that stock phrase further solidify her place in widowhood?

Then there had been church and the *really irritating* counseling by the Pastor's wife. Her heart was in the right place, for sure, but she could not help but feel a little resentful of her – in her ridiculous, stifflooking hat, bedazzled skirt suit, with her platitudes and her gleaming gold ring. What did she know of losing a husband? Or having to tell children who were way too young, that they had seen their father alive for the last time that morning? Had she ever had to tell a child who was terrified to go to sleep (because she equated sleeping with dying) to look for her daddy in her dreams? Or cried herself to sleep, knowing that the only reason all three children went to bed by 6 pm now, like clockwork, was to talk to their daddy in heaven?

It hadn't seemed real, talking with their lawyers, going over life insurance policies, land deeds, the will. "You had a good husband, Madam. Thanks to your late husband, you will be a very independently wealthy widow." That word again. *Widow*. Coupled with another word she despised, *late*. It just sounded disrespectful, like her husband had been tardy or something. Besides widows were her mother's peers - like Mrs. Ajulaka. She had been eight years old and had wondered why Mrs. Ajulaka was sitting on the floor, swathed in black. She could still recall the incessant wailing and the haunted eyes of Mrs. A's children, who also were her friends.

She had wanted to tell the pompous little lawyer man that before she was a 'Missus', she could have written her own ticket anyway, *thankyouverymuch*. But she knew that she was being overly sensitive, and really, what would that do besides make her seem like a bitchy, ungrateful widow? So instead, she lowered her eyes and looked appropriately grateful and demure. Yes, thank God for her wonderful husband-provider without whom she would be totally destitute. It felt wrong to be this angry, but there was no getting around it, she *was*.

She felt the most like shit on the days – yes, in the plural - when she did not especially feel like mourning. Grief was an emotion that permeated her being these days, but the act of mourning – well, there was a reason it was called an *act*. It took effort and energy, and frankly some of the rituals and expectations were exhausting, and some days to be honest, she just couldn't be bothered. *Let me grieve in peace*, she'd think to herself, too tired to affix the appropriate grieving widow expression on her face; hysterics today, forced numbness the next day. Oh, and the not eating was *killing* her! Sure, she hadn't felt like eating the first few days, but the expectation that she would go weeks and months without eating a proper meal was ludicrous. She looked resentfully at her 'ladies in mourning', her guests and sympathizers, as they shoveled food by the troughs into their mouths, in between crocodile tears. *I hope you all get grossly fat*, she thought to herself uncharitably, then stifled a giggle; another widow's no-no.

That first invitation had been hard; it had hit her like a punch to her gut. *To Mr. and Mrs. –*. She had been part of a unit so long that she had forgotten that this time, she'd be going alone. The expensive, linen card stock evoked a deep, primal loneliness within her. *No plus one.* She'd attended functions alone before, of course, but that was by choice. There would be no post-soirée dissection of their fellow revelers and their spousal dynamics – she would arrive alone, leave alone. Sit in the back of their chauffeur driven luxury car alone and climb into their king sized bed alone. At 6 pm now, whenever it was possible. *To talk to her husband in heaven.* Yes, she was a widow now.

{13}

The Fiancée

My fate was pretty much sealed on the first day we met. As I observed her through the side view mirror of Derek's car, something about her stance and the way her head was cocked (judgmentally, I thought) should have forewarned me that I was forever doomed to be categorized as the 'tiresome daughter-in-law,' to be tolerated, at best. I had dressed carefully for the occasion, in my sedate polka dot dress - small polka dots, so as not to appear tacky - accessorized with a thin red belt.

"You'll love my mother, she's such a fashionista, just like you." Derek had said, eyes twinkling. So dress to impress, I had surmised, grateful for some cue on what to expect from Derek's Mother. Ever since I had teased him about "overcompensating" because I was "African" and "hardly the kind of girl that he was expected to bring home to Mother," he had become deliberately nonchalant about his mother's preferences and what not, and had refused to offer even the tiniest tidbit of information to prepare me for meeting her.

"Nothing to prepare for, darling - you are perfect!" I loved him so much; he was so earnest and obviously trying (a little too hard in my opinion) not to appear to 'compensate'. It was endearing yet quite irritating, as it left me in the dark about the little unimportant details which we women know always turn out to be oh-so-important. Like the fiasco with the flowers - I found out too late that she thought all flowers except for white lilies and the occasional orchid were tacky and belonged at funerals. *Of course.* And my polka dot "number" as she referred to it, was not a hit; on its own it was "quite frumpy" and the patent leather belt was dismissed as "trying too hard."

She liked me even less as the tedious lunch wore on. "Your father is a King?" A slight smile hovered around those perfectly lined and filled-in lips. I remember thinking how impossibly thin her lips looked, like licorice - thin, pliable and red. "Well... not really, he's more like a titled chief, you see..." My voice trailed off under her amused stare.

"So you're not a princess then, are you?" Face serious, eyes mocking. "No, he's more like a political appointee..." I stuttered.

"Good – 'cause Derek and I are just common Polish immigrants. Aren't we, darling?"

Derek tried to convince me later that she was just kidding. Yeah, in a very weird, passive-aggressive, upper-class Caucasian way, I imagined.

"Loosen up, honey," he said, kissing my bare shoulders and rubbing my neck. It was the irony behind her words, rather than the words themselves, that stung. Marcia Gold, who happened to be as blueblood as they came, had married Derek's father, Aaron Gold, whose grandfather had changed his last name from Goldstein to the 'less immigrant sounding' Gold and had proceeded to make a fortune in the hotel business. The darned woman's forebears had probably come over on *The Mayflower* and she dared insinuate that I, the real immigrant here, *thankyouverymuch*, might be trying to put on airs!

Although it irked me to no end, I understood to a certain degree why she detested me. I was the direct antithesis of what she would consider a suitable wife for her precious Derek. I was so far off the mark that in the beginning I was secretly convinced that Derek was dating me just to rebel against his upbringing. I was not only a black African– but neither rich nor poor; my boring middle-class status must have been a huge disappointment.

How then could she 'sell' me? I was hardly the exotic refugee and certainly not the silver spoon bred 'princess of Zamunda.' Aside from being black, I didn't possess any traits or qualities that could potentially set me apart as a topic for some intriguing discussion at their country club.

I was, in her words (teach me to eavesdrop) "a complete and utter disaster."

"Give her a chance, honey. She'll come around." Derek made puppy dog eyes at me from across the room. "She's from a different era, my mother is." *More like another planet,* I thought to myself wryly. I was meeting Mrs. Gold (and yes, it was always *Mrs. Gold* by the way; never Marcie or, heaven forbid, Mom) at the dreaded country club, or as they referred to it 'The Enclave', to discuss the engagement party that she had insisted on throwing us.

"All white of course," she spoke in a firm yet unhurried tone.

"The flowers, or...?" I was confused, nervous, and very aware that I was out of my element here.

"...everything, naturally." This was not a response to my question, she had simply gone on speaking, as she was not requesting my input, she was *telling* me. I felt again chastised, as if somehow I should have known that at engagement parties, everything was always white -*naturally.*

"I just felt that I could incorporate some of my heritage into the event, with maybe more vibrant colors and maybe the décor..." My words sounded rushed and choked almost, resentment and emotions forming a large bubble in my throat.

She glanced at me for the first time that day, eyebrows cocked, superior smile in place.

"What, kente cloth and ostrich feathers? Somehow I don't see that fitting in at The Enclave..." She looked down at her notebook and adjusted her glasses.

"So, it's settled — white then..." she continued, speed bump steamrolled over, crisis averted. I could feel the tears well up behind my contact lenses. I was thirteen again, scared yet defiant, facing off against school bullies.

"Why don't you like me, Marcie?" I knew it was a mistake even as the words rolled off my tongue: I had just called her Marcie!

"Pardon me?" *You can stop this before it's too late; think of Derek*, I counseled myself. Yet I knew I wouldn't stop. *Couldn't.*

"You've never liked me or my kind from the first day you met me."

"Your kind?" her face still expressionless, "You mean... African?" Was she mocking me again?

It was hard to tell - I was emotional and she was a pro, well versed in the art of polite warfare.

"It just kills you that Derek loves me and will marry me regardless of what you think." The tears had started to fall, thick and heavy. Without looking down, she handed me a crisp white handkerchief (monogrammed, of course) from her crocodile skin purse, still studying me with a look I couldn't quite decipher.

"You don't sound too sure about that."

"I just want to be accepted for who I am." I was blubbering now.

"Your mascara is running." Okay, she was definitely toying with me now.

I charged on, pent up frustration finally let loose. "I know I never will be what you want..."

"Which is?" Face still implacable, I swear the woman had chilled Perrier water running through her veins.

"A friggin'... WASP!" She actually smiled at that, a slight upturn of her lips.

"No... it is safe to say you will never be." I stopped short, stung by the brevity of her response and matter of fact manner in which she said it.

"I'm not your problem dear, your issue is you." She broke off a piece of her croissant and delicately buttered it. "You must learn to be you in spite of me, or anyone else for that matter." For a minute I thought I had glimpsed some flicker of humanity under that veneer of icy Caucasian wealth and status.

"So...white it is then." My outburst had never happened.

{14}

The Jewel

*S*tomach in knots, clenched fists, tears in throat, pressure mounting behind eyes. *What am I gonna do, gonna do, gonna do?*
Silent scream, noiseless cry, storm filled clouds in my sky. Where can I go, can I go, can I go?
Suffocating, choking, can't breathe, can't stand, won't sit, don't lay, no comfort here.
Who can I tell, can I tell, can I tell?
Mind racing, rapid fire thoughts, internal conversations with myself. What I should have said, what I didn't say, what I held back, what I conceded to, what he labeled me. Where can I hide, can I hide, can I hide?
Pretty in pink on the outside – red bottomed shoes, Prada bag, gym toned abs, hair did, flashing smiles, dazzling ring, bling bling.

The Jewel

Colgate and Cartier but bruised, battered, ugly on the inside.

Who's gonna believe me, believe IN me, want me?

Diamond choker, choke hold grip. Diamond ring, gilded cuffs. McMansion, luxury car, picket fence, 2.5 babies – formulaic perfection.

Marital rape, emptiness, HIS bank account, HIS world – you just live in it.

Barbie doll, barbaric world, barber shop – wanna chop all this hair off,

wanna not be deceitfully picture perfect on the outside anymore.

You sold your soul for a diamond ring,

your heart and mind for fancy things.

Who you gonna tell, gonna tell, gonna tell?

King and Queen, let's play 'house'.

I'll be your boss, you'll be my spouse.

You wear what I buy, move where I say – you have an opinion, I'll make you pay.

Quiet as a mouse – ssshhhh.

Mortgage on the house – in too deep, cannot sleep, cannot swim. Private school, six years in.

Who's gonna save, gonna save, gonna save the day?

The rap on the glass broke her out of her reverie. "This is the happiest day of your life." *Or it should appear to be,* his look warned "You are turning forty, you're in Dubai with forty of your closest friends to celebrate. I did this," he paused for emphasis, "Just for *you*." He smiled with pride. She smiled through gritted teeth. "You did good, baby." Dutifully.

Mirror, mirror on the wall, who is the fakest?
Who is the weakest?
Who is the most dead inside?
Ice sculptures in Dubai, oasis in the desert but
drought in my heart. Lucky me, lucky her,
mirrored pill box in her purse. Vodka, razors,
overdose, how long before tub overflows?

Will she get to see his face as she slowly fades away? Hear him say, "Look what you did? Can't take you anywhere – can't even die right!" He'd scoff. What if she somehow survived? She stiffened with fear at the thought. It could quite possibly, be worse than death. He would have her committed for sure and then she would never see her kids again. At least dead she'd watch over them from heaven. Not like the useless figure head that she

The Jewel

was now. Rubberstamp mother – ask Dad for the real decision.

Padded cell, padded life,
 insulated in her strife.
The envy of the undiscerning, lusting eyes,
envying, yearning
for this life of hers that she would end tonight,
just as soon as she could wriggle out of this tight
designer dress. Lest there be forty more years just
like this.
Who would end this, end this, end this?
Wanna be me? Be like me? My nightmare is your
dream, so surreal it's true.
Complicated and unsimple,
out of this world but happening next door – that
neighbor a galaxy away. A cup of sugar from next
door, but the closest house is on Jupiter.
I need a friend, need help, need a friend.
She had married 'well', her Prince had found her.
Haha, the joke was on her.
Reverse zoo – animal on the outside, tamed in the
cage.
But it looks good though, the people have gotten
their money's worth.

Spectacle, splendor, spectacular, expensive,
unnecessary misery.
The price is dear, the priceless is cheap, loneliness
trumps penury. His 'jewel of inestimable value', he
boasts, she grimaces a smile, but they both know,
his jewel is a fake, he values her at zero.
Sotheby's jewel is a swap-meet find.
Thrifting, take me, buy me, antique me.
Anywhere but here, anywhere but here. Not here,
but nowhere.
Slashed wrists, wine sedated, birthday cake, most
sated.
Show n tell for scars, the most 'hurting-est' wins –
she got this. Show me your 'boo-boo' and I'll show
you mine.
 Band-Aid ripped off, bloody, but internal wounds
much deeper. Hurt better, more secret,
in the morning light disbelieved.
 Liar, liar, pants on fire, it was so bad, so dire,
yet you sat there, unbound?
But not quite free – bought with currency so cheap
(rubles, lira, cowries, now defunct) that we do not
speak of it.
Except on pretend paper and invisible ink,

fear of being found out paramount – must not
topple the bride from cake.
Cake fights only fun in movies, messy in real life.
Dry cleaning bills, catering bills, gossiping guests
with averted eyes. Bride cries, mother cries,
groom so mad, ooh he mad!
Fear: cost of cake way too dear
and value of her life not high enough – it does not
outweigh the shame.
You let us down, you spilled the beans.
You ain't the first, won't be the last, but so
indiscreet.
Tsk Tsk.
You should have let them eat cake. But it's ruined
now.
My bad, my fault, ALL my fault.

Let them grace our gala of destruction in their
finery from Neiman Marcus and Bloomies. They
have earned their right to dine on the debris of our
union, chewing up fragments of children who will
grow up thinking that this is how it has to be, cars
and houses that will soon be not just theirs but
'communal property'.

"Toast your love," they say and he does. She looks on through unseeing eyes, a clenched jaw and her perpetual noiseless scream.

No love here except for the fight.
Bound by battle, enemies on the same side,
fighting for the right to keep fighting
each other to the death.
Misery loves company and so
I got you babe.
 I got you, I got you, I got you.

{15}

The Trip

It was early evening as they both watched the sun creep beneath the clouds, slowly, magnified it seemed by the large airport window. Lost in their separate thoughts, they held hands, unified in their reluctance to have the conversation that they knew was inevitable.

"I will miss this," he said, stooping to drop a kiss at the top of her head. She smiled, a slight tug of her lips, and snuggled closer to him. *Me too*, she thought, but said instead "Even with those beautiful American girls?" Her tone sounded jealous and needy even to her own ears. She winced inwardly as she anticipated his withdrawal.

"We've been over this a thousand times," He spoke in that patient, yet condescending manner that he knew she detested. "Mugo, don't...it came out wrong..." She plucked at his sleeve, avoiding the anger that she knew would be in his eyes." I just don't want us to be like..." She paused, as a sob caught in her throat.

"Like your ex-boyfriend." He had firmly and coolly removed her hand from his sleeve, facing her squarely now. "I don't know what to say – what do I have to do to show you that I am not Eric? This is why I didn't want to accept any money from you - in fact here..." He tried to place the crisp dollars in her limp hands, turning away as they fell like leaves to the floor.

She watched him walk away, her heart breaking with every step he took. Mugo had walked further down to the almost empty airport seating lounge, and was staring out the window, brooding. Through the corner of her eye, she watched him retrace his steps, trailing his hand on the side of the window, in a childlike manner, as he walked. She knew what he would do before he reached her. *Don't pick it up*, she pleaded silently, *please don't, let this be different, lord*. She watched him stoop to one knee, showing a flash of his navy blue socks as he nonchalantly picked up the money that lay splayed out, fan-like on the filthy airport carpet. She couldn't stop the tears as he came towards her, the sickening déjà vu even more tangible. What was it about her, she had often wondered that attracted these types of men?

She was nice to look at, smart, with a good head on her shoulders, but it seemed like every man she had ever dated took advantage of whatever she had to offer at the time, leaving her emotionally and sometimes financially drained. Like Eric. She remembered how sick to her stomach she had been when she found out that there had never been any scholarship, never been any plans to return. And here she was, five years later, doing it all over again. "Look honey," He was being patronizing she knew, "in about an hour, I'm going to get on that plane. Let us enjoy this time and see it as a celebration of our future and not, *this*..." He gestured towards her face that was still damp with tears.

"Give it back." She had barely spoken above a whisper, but from his expression, she knew he heard her. "My money, I want it back." Her voice was firm, made louder by her confidence in her decision, abrupt as it was. "You said you never wanted it- you love me for me, right?"

She faced him squarely, watching him as he swallowed and nodded, yet still remaining frozen, staring at her outstretched hand. She slid his wallet from his coat pocket and deliberately counted out the thousand dollars she had given him, ten crisp hundred dollar notes. Her smile was genuine this time when she saw the slackened 'O' that his mouth had become.

"Good bye and good luck, sweetie." She paused for emphasis," I'll wait for you." She turned and walked away from him, confident and sure footed, out of the dreary airport and into the warm night air.

{16}

The Thief

The crowd had started to boo and jeer. Nneoma felt a ripple of something - not fear, but close - adrenalin maybe, start to course down her spine. She was soaked with sweat in the nearly one hundred degree weather, but she felt cold, the chill probably radiating from her clammy hands to the rest of her lithe, petite body.

They would not be kind to her, she knew. The average trader despised her 'type' as a rule. The men for sure, found it irritating that pretty, university student girls like her were mostly snooty and unattainable, but it was the women, indeed her very own 'gender-kin', who would take the most pleasure in picking her skin - soft, supple and yellow as it was - from its very bones, if the opportunity presented itself. They circled her, hissing and spitting scornfully in the ochre colored dust. *Like hyenas*, she thought, *just like a pack of hungry, cowardly hyenas*. It was difficult to imagine feeling superior, perched as she was on her throne of shame, amidst the market rubble and partially disintegrated plastic bags that had become enmeshed into the packed soil, the product of years of litter, months of rain and the steady tread of sellers and customers, but somehow she managed. She kept a slightly supercilious smile on her face – not too cocky, but just enough to show that she was above all this and something in her posture indicated that surely they knew this was a mistake, a ridiculous accusation and it would soon all be sorted out.

*** *** ***

The day had begun like any other week day. She had woken up next to Eze's warmth and had nestled against him, breathing in his scent while willing herself to get out of bed. She was already in front of the mirror braiding her hair into her signature style, two long plaits on either side of her face, when Eze awoke. He sat in bed quiet, drinking her in, in that manner he had, that made her go weak in the knees. He loved her hair that way, he always told her, like a school-girl, innocent and honest. She had always laughed at that, his description of her hair as honest, as if her strands somehow were imbued with moral character.

And now she was here, barely two hours later, sitting on the cement blocks that created a makeshift dais in the middle of the marketplace. She no longer wore her prim red blazer as it had been torn in the scuffle, one long sleeve now hanging by threads. She had folded it neatly and used it as a cushion, dignified in this moment of utter humiliation and chaos. "*Ole!*" someone shouted. Thief. She remained still and calm, braiding the plait that had come undone, possibly when one of the vicious 'hyena-women' had yanked at her hair. She had refused to fight them, holding firm to her status as the educated one amidst a bunch of savages. She hoped her posture and attitude reflected the boredom and scorn that she was desperately trying to project.

They had descended on her like a flock of bees, their filthy hands raiding her most sacred parts, under the guise of searching her. Dozens of hands raked at her breasts and the more daring had tried to rally support to pull off her underwear.

"I am on my period." She spoke without embarrassment, her voice devoid of any emotion. A hasty consensus was reached, no one was willing to 'touch the dirty whore', but a few die-hard women had insisted that she "show them."

"I will need another tampon." She said flatly, gesturing as if to remove her underwear, and they hesitated, distaste winning over their figurative thirst for blood.

"We suppose burn am." For the first time, fear welled up like a nauseous gas in her stomach. It rarely happened in this particular market; the burning of thieves, but the crowd was hostile and she had no obvious sympathizers.

"Nooooo... how much wey she steal we go come burn am? Person pikin?" The uproar started again, some arguing that the monetary value determined if and when burning was necessary, and in this case it was not. The shop owner on the other hand, argued that it was the principle that mattered. Today, a bottle of nail polish; tomorrow, armed robbery. She relaxed inwardly; face still expressionless, willing Eze to drive by, as he usually did, on his way to work. She knew he would not see her, but the throng of people had spilled onto the street and impeded the flow of traffic and so she hoped that he would be forced to get down and take a look.

*** *** ***

By the time Eze arrived, she was numb from sitting so stiffly and her eyes stung from the sweat that had run into her eyes as she stared unseeing, at the sea of people before her. He had pushed through the crowd, policemen in tow, and scooped her off the cement blocks and into his arms like a baby. His face was tense, angry. During the drive home, he said nothing to her, staring straight ahead, as if to will the traffic away. "Nneoma, you promised." His voice sounded husky and broken, like he had been crying almost.

"And I kept my promise - I didn't do it Eze, I swear." His eyes searched hers, seeking evidence that she was telling the truth. "I swear. On our unborn child." She held her breath until she saw him relax, he knew that she would never defile something so innocent, so pure.

"I'm going to work now. Get some rest, okay?" He was half whistling as he walked towards his car, grateful for her ready denial, relieved that the ordeal was over with. Nneoma watched him from the window as he backed out of the driveway.

Inhaling deeply, she reached into the waistband of her demure white panties and felt the inevitable wetness there. The release was instantaneous; the adrenalin gave her a headiness that defied logic. She finally exhaled and instinctively cast a quick look around the bedroom, as if she expected Eze to pop out from behind the dresser.

Satisfied that she was alone, she extricated the clear nail varnish from 'down there', placed it on the nightstand and began to file her nails.

{17)

The Writer

Her father had been her first critic. He had taught creative writing in a community college for many years, and had worked on his 'masterpiece' novel since she could remember. "My Dad is a writer," she would tell her friends at school. It sounded way fancier than 'professor', even to her back then. "Ooh," her friend Lynette was easily impressed, "like Stephen King?" "Better," she'd said proudly. "Yeah? What's the name of his book?" Barry had asked. She didn't like Barry; he was a big bully who always seemed to be sweating, even first thing in the morning. "Um, um..." she stuttered. He threw back his head and laughed. "Liar, liar, pants on fire. Neka's a liiiiiiii-aaaaaarrrrrrrr!" Tears welled up in her eyes and Lynette, her best friend, had sidled up to her and slipped her hand in hers. "I believe you. I'm gonna ask my Mom if we can buy your Daddy's book." Neka had nodded. This time the tears in her throat were of gratitude.

There was no book, though; at least not yet. She had asked her Father tentatively, later, when he would be done with his book, and he had all but exploded at her. "You children don't understand the sacrifices I make for this family! You think I want to be teaching these dim wits all day? You think I don't want to finish my book? Nonsense." He had spent that weekend locked in his study with a typewriter, reams of paper, and scotch. As an adult, Neka had often wondered if her father was a frustrated alcoholic who wrote, or a frustrated writer that drank. But at least he was a docile drunk. And drinking and his novel draft was all he had, she theorized, besides a wife who did not share or understand his artistic aspirations, two children, and a less than stellar career.

The first and last time she had shown him her writing she had been thirteen or fourteen years old. She'd been writing here and there, but she knew that this poem was special. It had been something like 'Déjà vu, here's thinking about you...' She had felt that this was her masterpiece—mature and mysterious; her friends were still writing 'roses are red, violets are blue,' for Pete's sake. He had read it and said, "Kema wrote this? No? I'd always figured Kema for the writer." But he had kept it in his file, where he kept his 'very important papers' and she had glowed with pride. One day, after one of his drunken writing episodes, she had peeped at the sheet in his typewriter and there it was; her entire poem, word for word. Neka didn't know whether to feel pride, or shame for her father, or both. What kind of person plagiarized his own child's work? Even though she knew his book would never be finished, or published, she still wished that he hadn't done it.

And later, when she had mentioned wanting to be a writer and her father had discouraged her saying, "You want to be like me? Can you not learn from my mistakes?" she had said to herself, *but I'm not you, I'm better than you.* Out loud however, she had said, "Those that can't do, teach." She had regretted it as soon as she had said it, of course; after that things had never been the same between them. That was the day that they ceased to be father and daughter, and became rivals; like two writers fighting for the last pen on earth.

In college, when her writing teacher had been blatantly obvious in her preference for another student's writing, and person in general, it had been hard for Neka to swallow. She was nine, fourteen, seventeen, again; and Ms. Carrie was her father. 'People who can't do, teach' was on the tip of her tongue, but she was wiser now, more mature. The best short story from the workshop was traditionally chosen by the fellow members of the class, critiqued, and submitted to the annual 'So you think you can write' contest. It was subject to the teacher's discretion, but to Neka's knowledge, no teacher had ever exercised their veto power until now. She had been hurt and stunned all at once— she knew Ms. Carrie thought Brandon was the best thing since sliced bread, but was her writing so bad, or Brandon's so great, that Ms. Carrie would go against the whole class? Especially since Brandon himself, had voted for her.

"So, you honestly think Brandon is the better writer?"

Ms. Carrie's tone had been even keeled and neutral, as if she was used to being confronted by audacious students every day. "No, I don't. His story isn't even as good as yours, to be honest. But he wrote the best story he could, and it is adequate; good, even."

"But mine was better!" She was indignant now.

"But not your best, and that in my opinion makes you undeserving of the opportunity to even compete. You could win the competition with it, sure. But that would keep you from ever progressing any further—your sort gets comfortable with the first writing style that works. Frankly, I prefer Brandon's style, but that's just my opinion. I do recognize that you are the superior writer, Neka—but it's just not your time, sorry." And that had been that. Brandon hadn't won, but had received honorable mention, and Neka always remembered feeling robbed, and not a little resentful of Ms. Carrie. She had just never understood the lesson there, or agreed that there was one to be learned.

The Writer

Our people say that when the sun shines, and the heavens leak water, a light persistent drizzle, simultaneously, a baby leopard has been born somewhere. And many years ago, when the eclipse came, they said a great man had died. He was one of the heavenly bodies, thus the sun would not– nay, could not–in deference to the passing of so great a man, shine its light. I often wondered, but never spoke it out loud; what happens when a great woman dies? There was no precedent for such a foretelling; as if the phrase itself were a contradiction in terms.

"Um, yeah–no. This ain't it, boo." Xavier shook his head while looking at her over his horn rimmed 'hipster' glasses. "I mean, it's a nice piece, but the whole 'lions and tigers' shit? Americans do not want to read that–unless they are like nine years old. Even then, it's a maybe." He softened his tone just a tad, "You bring me a STORY. More *Americanah*, less Lion King. Something current– that immigrants in America can relate to." He raked his fingers through his curls, frustrated, yet trying not to lay into her too much. He liked the girl; he just knew that she was capable of writing so much better than all this horribly clichéd shit.

"I mean, come on! You're American with Nigerian parents; you have the unique advantage of being in this niche now, while the perspective of the first generation immigrant is hot. I suggest you seize this opportunity—that is, if you are still trying to put this book out. With me." And with the not so subtle threat hanging in the air, he turned away from her, towards his floor to ceiling windows, leaned back in his chair, and closed his eyes. One sided meeting over. Neka sighed, picked up her leather laptop case and said wearily, "I'll show myself out then." He didn't respond but she hadn't expected a response anyway. As much as she hated to admit it, he was right; she had not delivered her best. She was writing for who she thought her audience was, instead of just writing and letting her audience find her. A friend from her writing class had told her once, "What if your audience doesn't know they are your audience yet? Or what if they haven't even been born or discovered you at that time?" At first, she'd laughed it off, like he was just trying to be deep, but later she'd turned it over in her mind. Yeah, did Dostoevsky, Tolstoy and 'em know or care that a Nigerian girl would be reading and loving their work a century later? Should they have been swayed by the possibility or dissuaded by the lack thereof? Nope. And neither would she, she had promised herself.

*** *** ***

I get up from the bed with a start, nudged awake by the uncomfortable damp spot—a badge of our illicit lovemaking. Silently, but deliberately, I begin to dress. Tunic over head, leggings over hips, flats on feet, thong in purse. Who am I? My lips twist wryly as I tiptoe out the door, looking back for a final glance at Jacques, my lover, as he sleeps, arm flung over his eyes, and the other still curved where I was nuzzled up to him just a few minutes ago.

"Oh what a tangled web we weave," I mutter under my breath to myself, even as my eyes fall on the tangled mess of his taupe bed linens. Yes, I am the mistress of played out irony. Lover of the staggeringly handsome Jacques. Wife of- well, not Jacques. It is a peculiar relationship we have, my

husband and I. He needs me, and I need to be needed by him- together we are the ultimate cliché. But we have weathered so much together! His alcoholism, my miscarriages; his unemployment, my depression. We owe it to our marriage counselors and therapists, if only for not to have wasted their time, and our money. It seems sad, written in black and white like that, but it really isn't that bad. There is more that binds us than separates, and I for one am not ready to, or even capable of making this exhausting journey with anyone else; or making it again, for that matter.

He thinks that this is a sign, of course. 'We are made for each other. No other couple in the world could go through what we have been through and still be...us. You know?' I know. Like I said, I wouldn't do this with anyone else, but I do know that we do not have the healthiest of relationships.

Jacques says I'm his soul mate too. Poor kid. I kind of understand his rationale. I mean, why else would I be jeopardizing my marriage to be with him, he must wonder. "You are meant for me.

We are meant for each other." He says this after sex one day, as we share a cigarette, blowing rings of smoke up at the ceiling, circa 1800 B.C. Again, who am I? I almost groan with disbelief—what, has he been meeting up with my husband for coffee or something? I'm uncomfortable enough with the situation without the hearts and flowers stuff. I turn on my side and mumble some endearment that means nothing to me, but everything to my infatuated Lothario. But I think to myself how convenience has more to do with it, than any kind of destiny.

"May I offer you some advice as a woman?" Kema's body language—squared, stiff shoulders, the vigorous jangling of her bracelets (arm candy as she called them)—suggested that this was a rhetorical question. "Not as your sister, not even as an editor. Do not sell your soul for this," she gestured scornfully, "this—crap! It is simply not worth it."

"What do you mean?" Neka was truly confused.

"Oh, you know what I mean, Neks!" Kema was tapping her pen on the edge of the desk, almost in perfect time to her rising agitation level, it seemed. What was she so mad about, Neka wondered?

"You're gonna mess around and screw things up with Aaron." Kema was almost vibrating, she seemed so angry.

"Whoa. What has Aaron got to do with anything?" Neka was completely bewildered, now. "Oh, come on, Neks, Aaron is not stupid and neither am I. Jacques is ol' dude you had that thing with," she held up her hand to silence Neka's protest, "and the chick in this piece is you. It would be foolish and hurtful to publish this. Just my 'uninformed' opinion." She used air quotes.

Neka shook her head in a mixture of shock and bafflement. That 'thing' had been a silly flirtation with a random dude—nothing had come of it. It had been inappropriate but harmless; moreover, she and Aaron had been on a break and they had decided that since they had both been 'doing their own thing', it was really no biggie. Plus, they weren't married, or even talking marriage. "Kems, I swear, sometimes I think no one knows me better than you in this world, and other times I am certain you haven't a clue who I am." She adjusted her scarf and got up. "I'm so done; I couldn't convince you and I really do not have the energy to try today." She paused at the door, "But at least be woman enough to admit to yourself that this isn't about Aaron; or me, for that matter. You know who this is really about."

"Wait." All the fury seemed to have seeped out of Kema like a deflated balloon. "You're right." Neka slowly and warily made her way back to one of the overstuffed chairs. "As usual. And your timing sucks donkey balls- as usual." They both laughed a little at that. "It's just that I literally just told Robert about the Ricardo thing last week." She rolled her eyes in mock exasperation at herself and at Neka's incredulous expression. "I know, girl, I know. I wasn't going to, as you are well aware, but we kind of are starting things over, clean slate, etcetera etcetera, so I-" she broke off, "so when I read your piece- this 'Jacques shit'- it was like a punch to the gut."

Neka's mouth was dry and her head was spinning. No, Kema, she thought wryly, your timing sucks. "So what are you saying? This is like the only story my editor even likes at this point."

Kema came over and sat on the arm of her chair. "What am I saying? What I'm saying baby sis, is this; publish what you want, but this could really mess things up for me. Really, really badly."

*** *** ***

She was meeting with Louanne again, and she had no idea why she had even suggested that they have coffee. Louanne was one of those friends that one was both awed and intimidated by. You knew she battled something within her that made her innately bitchy, and you knew that today could be your day to bear the brunt of it, but if you were lucky and she validated you that day, it was worth it. Pathetic, yes, but nevertheless she had paid particular attention to her outfit—wearing her only pair of Louboutins and a crisp white blouse, to go with a midi peplum skirt, when she dressed to meet Louanne for coffee. Or caffeine, as Lou called it. "You're late," Neka teased her, as Lou wafted in—

and she was, but she was beautiful, and so used to being exempt from most social graces, it was somewhat charming. "I am also de-caffeinated." She air kissed Neka and held up a hand to wave the waiter towards her, "Caffeine, darling. With lots of froth and tons of cinnamon. Thank you!" She smiled brightly, charming the pants off the waiter and Neka simultaneously.

She only took her sunglasses off when they were done with their coffee and she was nursing a large icy frappucino. "So, the book, dahling- what gives?" Lou had dated a French film director years ago, and was now, by extension, French. "Well, did you read what I sent you?" Neka asked. Lou had spent a lot of time with influential writers, publishers, and the like, and so Neka really valued her opinion on these things. "No," Lou shook her silver flecked bun regretfully, "I skimmed it though, and it looked good." Neka was relieved; it seemed Lou was in a benevolent mood. "I mean, we all know you can write, Neka, that's not the point; YOU just have to believe it."

"Um, well, thanks, I guess." Neka swallowed hard, she was particularly nervous about showing any vulnerability to Lou, because she automatically went for the jugular. "I need your advice on something. Someone close to me has asked me not to publish one of my stories, as it could adversely affect this person. What should I do?"

Lou studied her for a moment and then said," First off, both of you are assuming way too much; you, that you'll be published, and this person, that the book will sell, and that anyone would read it and make the connection." She laughed–a short bark. "Narcissistic, much?" Neka almost snorted at that, since Lou was one of the biggest narcissists she knew. She was stung though, by Lou's dismissiveness of her work and the impact it could potentially have. "I beg your pardon? I have a publisher-" Lou was unfazed by her indignation. "Ah yes, the little indie publisher that could." She was more amused than scornful, "Let's be honest, it's practically self-publishing." Yes, Louanne could be a bitch.

"You can be such a nasty person, Lou," Neka blurted out before she could stop herself.

"Yet, here we are." She was smiling, but her eyes were not. "I don't know what you *should* do, but this is what I would do; I would write and tell my story exactly as I'd planned. What I wouldn't do, however, is publish with some rinky dink publisher. But then again, I am a nasty bitch, right?"

Later that evening, Neka was wondering why she let Louanne do this to her; why she sought her validation even though she knew Lou was mean and incapable of such. Maybe she responded to the nuggets of truth that Lou dished out. Louanne was mercilessly frank. True, she had many demons. She had been used and abused by almost every male figure in her life from very early on; from her step-father, who'd sent her to expensive boarding schools in exchange for his inappropriate groping, to a teacher in boarding school who'd sensed her vulnerability and had zeroed in like most predators, mentoring and molesting her simultaneously. Then there had been bosses and powerful men, whom Lou had tried to convince herself she controlled, but who actually used her. So in return she lorded her hard earned connections over her friends. She had never learned how to trust or love anyone, so she charmed and abused them alternately; the carrot and the stick—she had learned that well, but knew nothing else.

*** *** ***

Writing was a lot like love, and a good story akin to a lover—the obsession, the draw—no matter what your friends said, you went back for more. Neka knew what stories would make the cut, in spite of the editors, her sister, Lou, her own insecurities—the ones that wrote themselves, practically, that gave her chills when she reread them for the umpteenth time, wanting a reason to loathe them, to critique them; the stories that were so good, they got better each time she read them. Sometimes she would read them out loud to herself, marveling at the way the words floated off her tongue, as if they had been strung together by someone much more talented than herself. The ones with the clever word play and nuances that she hoped her someday readers would get; the same way she prayed that their belly would mimic the flip that hers did when she knew that she had written something so honest, so accurate that it had to resonate with somebody, *somewhere*–touch a young girl maybe; make her want to write and want to evoke that feeling in someone else that way. A good writer chose her stories with care and much agonizing, but if you were lucky, ever so often, one would choose you. This one had chosen her.

Panting heavily, mud, leaves and twigs plastered to my body like indecent, filthy, macramé art, I run through the forest; heart pounding, chest heaving, thighs slippery with my own juices, no longer contained by my underwear, my panty liner.

I pause and incline my ear to the sound of my own fear, my rapidly beating heart; afraid to breathe, my body twisted at an insane angle, like some lithe, feral animal. Prey. I am being hunted. Survival instinct in full gear, dignity a thing of the past, I clamber up a tree as quietly as I can, in the pitch black night. The bark, the ants, make short work of my delicate nether regions. I do not budge for hours, having schooled myself to breathe in an irregular pattern, as if my pursuers are armed with breath-tracking devices. But it is the only thing I have control over, and it calms me in some strange, almost yogic way. Deep breaths, through my nostrils, small, silent releases through my mouth, two short puffs in quick succession. Over and over again, until I am lulled to sleep by my own breathy lullaby.

Crackle. I am awakened by a noise. An animal? A footstep, maybe? I freeze–ready to kill or be killed.

"Sister." It is a whisper; that of one who wishes to be heard by only the person she wishes to be heard by. Me. I wait, to make sure that she has not been followed by them. After a beat or two, I allow the relief to flood my body and my breathing to return to normal.

"Sister," I respond, my voice husky with emotion, with lack of use, with thirst. Instantly, a light is shone on me. "She's here," sister says, her voice emotionless and flat, "I found her; she's here." Our eyes meet, identical almost, except one holds fear, the other extreme loathing. All at once, I am falling and falling and falling, a silent scream in my head, eyes shut. How could I have climbed

that high? I do not remember. Ah, forgive me, sister...

ACKNOWLEDGEMENTS

The self publishing route is viewed by many as a self-aggrandizing, vanity project of sorts, and (true or not) can be quite a lonely choice, devoid of guidance and validation from agents, editors and publishers, so I am especially grateful for my behind the scenes coterie of encouragement on my journey. 2015 EDIT: I am happy to revise this to state that for this revised edition, this was so NOT the case. I am beyond grateful and blessed to add Abra Lyman, my friend and unofficial editor of this book, to the list. She invested weeks of her time to bring my manuscript to the level she thought it should be. And all I can say is, "Oh my." What a 'level' of perfection it is! Also, to Carol Gachiengo, for making four of these stories that much better.

Special mention still goes to the following:

My sister, Chi-Chi, for making me want to write at a pretty young age, and in adulthood, when I no longer wanted to write - insisting that my short stories were worthy of publication and being read by a wider audience. My good friend (*ufan*), Ekaette, for her daily encouragement and being there to bounce off ideas *ad nauseum*- thank you for always responding to my crazy freaking out texts.

Friends and family, thank you! My readers and fans that graciously reviewed my book on Amazon (some of which I have featured in this book), I love you ALL! Thank you to Gotham Writers Workshop, where several of these stories were born; My talented cover designer, Sara Capooter – You GET me. Welcome and thank you to any new fans I may gain, to those that follow StorySheWrote on Facebook www.fb.com/StorySheWrote; I hope we become family, soon. If you enjoyed 'The Hawker', I have a treat for you – in the form of a comic book adaptation of it by the talented Adeniran Adeniji and his team. It is available on Amazon (Kindle) for just .99 cents and it is titled 'Love & Mangoes" by CC Adetula. Enjoy!

Lastly, and certainly not the least, to the greatest things I ever made, my three perfect children, and the man I made and raise them with.

Thank you for the support and not whining too much when I was ignoring you guys and fiddling with my computer. We did it!☺

For updates about my new work coming out in 2016, join the discussion on our FB page or email us at storyshewrotemedia@gmail.com to be added to our mailing list!

Books are on Amazon, On Kindle and in Nigeria – hard copies can be found at:

Terra Kulture - Plot 1376, Tiamiyu Savage, Off Ahmadu Bello Way, Victoria Island, Lagos.

234-1-2700-588

Or

The Novel Stand – 25 Nelson Mandela Street, Off Bassey Duke Street, Calabar, Cross River State 08037874460

Also available for download on www.okadabooks.com